The Lost Journal

A Record of the
Mischief, Mayhem, Madness and Magic of an
unlikely Brotherhood of Nine-year-old
Boys in the late 1960s

by

James D Marshon

GREY COURT PRESS

Contents

Introduction

How this book came to be written

This book started with an ill-judged decision to visit my dad. He was a hundred-and-two years old. So, I flew back to that small village outside Manchester where I grew up. Soon after my arrival, even before offering me tea, he ordered me to clear my things out of the attic. I suppose it wasn't an unreasonable request. After all, they had been there for over fifty years. I didn't want to do this, so I had to think fast and devise a plan. I closed the window and surreptitiously turned up the gas fire. It wouldn't be long now; no one hundred-and-two year old man could resist the stifling warmth of the room. Hopefully, he would soon nod off, after which I would escape and be back at the hotel with my feet up, sipping a glass of cabernet and ordering room service.

As usual, with my best-laid plans, it was not to be. The old man had outwitted me. Amped up on copious amounts of caffeinated tea, ginseng, and wearing his old horsehair vest, he was able to fight off the urge to doze. He had anticipated my trickery. "I was born at night," he said, "but not last night. You learn to stay awake in the army," he declared proudly. "I got a commendation from my commanding officer for always being alert."

"I didn't know the Duke of Wellington gave out commendations," I remarked, but I didn't have a chance to finish the sentence as his walking stick rapped the arm of my chair. "Get up those bloody stairs he yelled," and off I went as usual. It wasn't the first time I had heard those words; I never thought I would still be hearing them at my age.

I went up the stairs and pulled down the ladder leading to the dreaded trap door and the attic. All the while, the words of Gandalf the Grey were echoing in my head: "There are fouler things than Orcs in the dark places of this world." That attic was a very dark place. It was rumoured that my brother had left some old underwear in there that had continued to fester unnaturally for decades, hoping to spontaneously combust into life like something from a Stephen King novel. I climbed the steps and pushed open the trap door with my back as I held a crucifix in one hand and my dad's bread knife in the other. I was not going to be taken unawares.

The attic was dark, forbidding, and thick with dust. The musty air smelled damp and more than a little unnatural. At the back of the attic was a large old cedar box. I opened the box tentatively, praying that it wasn't the same box that had been under my dad's bed fifty years ago. I had only just finished paying for the years of therapy incurred by that experience. Much to my relief it wasn't.

There was all kinds of stuff in that attic. There was my brother's trumpet from his high school band years; I knelt down and instinctively tested the padlock to see if it was still secure after my dad had chained the offending instrument to the floor, lest my brother ever decide to come looking for it.

My old copy of War and Peace was on the table. That book profoundly impacted me during my high school years, as it propped up my bed after the bottom right leg broke off while I was engaged in a homework assignment with Belinda Effington. Hiding beneath a stack of old football programs, record albums, and comic books was my old report card from St Matthews, the pages now fading yellow and crumpled. My parent's tear stains were still evident, reminders of when my dad wept uncontrollably upon realising the enormity of his unmet expectations. Yes, there were the dirty eraser marks and pin scrapes, where the official grades had been replaced by a scrawled nine-year-old's attempt to replace an F with a clumsy A. I couldn't help reflecting on how a career as a forger would not have ended well for me.

That should have been it, except that there, half hidden in the corner under a stack of old holiday brochures touting two weeks on the Costa del Sol for five pounds ten shillings, was an old red notebook with Jimmy's Journal written across the front. I picked it up gingerly, dusted it off, and began flipping through the pages. It was chock full of writing. This was my old journal from primary school. It was all coming back to me as I gazed at the nine-year-old scrawl filling page after page. We had been given the project of journalling all the significant things that happened to us each month, whether at school, home, or out and about with the lads during the school year 1967-68. Here it all was, written in some form of juvenile hieroglyphics.

I sat on a stool in that dusty attic and began to read. Opening that book was like entering a time portal. I was instantly swept back into a different world, that I thought had dissolved forever into the ether of time. In that dusty attic I reconnected with that boy I had known in another life. Not only him but friends, family, and acquaintances, many of whom were now long gone. This catalyst ignited my quest to translate those nine-year-old scribblings and bring them to life once more. In so doing, I was able to revisit that world of mischief, mayhem, madness, and magic that I had known in those golden days of boyhood. After reading the journal for herself, my publisher insisted I share it in the form of this book. Here it is. The journal recaptures not just a year in my life, but also the shifting societal values so colourfully expressed by the psychedelic counterculture revolution of a changing world. The journal had lain in the dust, undisturbed and forgotten for over half a century. This book is an account of that journal, recalling all those crazy exploits as they happened to me, and the unlikely brotherhood of nine-year-old boys I called my friends. Framed through the lens of a man who has lived the rest of that boy's life, the journal reflects so many experiences that are common to every generation. This book is based on actual events and real people, whose names I have changed for fear of being hunted down by an angry mob of senior citizens.

September 1967

Chapter 1
Those Who Are About to Die

———◆◇◆———

The dog days of August were gone, taking with them the last real heat of the summer. It was September 1967, and the ominous shadow of school hung over us like the proverbial harbinger of doom. It was not long before I found myself back in the schoolyard with the rest of the lads, lamenting the fact that, as Beaky informed us, there were 105 days, 15 hours, and 45 minutes until the Christmas holidays.

The first of the journal entries describes the first week of September that year as sunny and bright, even if our collective mood was not. The lads had congregated in our usual meeting place behind the bike sheds. We caught up on all the events of the past summer, including all the latest news about football, cricket, and family holidays.

Eventually, the conversation took a different course as we honed in on Cynthia Hardcastle's new hairstyle. Of course, we all agreed in a very unconvincing and most disingenuous way that it was quite hideous. Cynthia Hardcastle was a living dream, and every boy's secret crush, but our gang law strictly forbade fraternising with girls. In fact, it was our Prime Directive, initiated to prevent us from accidentally straying into the alien realm of Girlworld, a place, according to my dad, where you relinquished all rights to the rest of your life.

While we feigned disinterest and dismissive intolerance of those strange and intoxicating creatures, they did seem to have a massively disarming effect on us. Well, when I say all of us, there was one exception: Georgie Lightfoot. Georgie was our hero when it came to girls; he seemed to possess a secret superpower that made him somehow immune and invulnerable to all their feminine charms and wiles.

Not the least of these strange and largely incomprehensible beings was Cynthia Hardcastle, who had a stranger effect than most girls, as she was a grade A bona fide goddess, whose mere presence made you forget how to talk and caused your left leg to shake uncontrollably. Cynthia had auburn hair and brown eyes, like two deep dark pools that a small boy could so easily fall into and helplessly drown. Best of all, though, she smelled of vanilla.

It wasn't long before the conversation turned from girls to another devastating and equally destructive force: nuclear missiles. This was 1967, and the Cold War was still raging. Every night on the BBC, we listened in to discover what the Russians were up to. I asked my dad what to do if they did launch an attack on us. My dad, ever the undying optimist, would say, "Well, if they do attack, the best thing to do, Jimmy, is to bend over, place your head between your legs, and kiss your..." It would be years before I discovered what it was I was supposed to kiss goodbye, because my mother would interrupt him loudly and with undisguised horror. She would then send me upstairs to go and wash my neck. What good would a clean neck do if an atomic bomb hit our house?

Back behind the bike sheds Billingsley was in full flow declaring that the Russians had 3,000 long-range nuclear missiles all aimed at Britain. It all sounded very drastic, and we whistled ominously. Billingsley thought of himself as the fount of all knowledge; he had a very large apple-shaped head, which was circled by a mop of dishwater blond hair that hung limply down over an impressively large forehead, beneath which were piggy eyes, and a large protruding nose, all of which perched on an unusually narrow neck. If William Tell had sired an older and less fortunate son, it would have been Billingsley. He had an opinion about everything and stated it with annoying regularity. There was just one minor problem. It wasn't that Billingsley was always completely and totally wrong about everything, it was just that he came really close.

I was lost in thought: 3,000 nuclear missiles all aimed at us. I mean, where would they all go? It seemed like a lot of rockets, unless you were planning on nuking places like Grasmere, St Asaph's, or Cherry Hinton.

Mikey brought me back to reality by asking us where we thought the safest place to go would be in case of a nuclear attack. "Arthur Scargill's house," said Beaky with confidence.

"MI6 headquarters," said Mikey, "that would be safe as they would never bomb their own people."

Billingsley suggested that Liverpudlians would probably be the safest, because they had all lived so close to the River Mersey for so long, they would be immune to any nuclear fallout.

"My Uncle Sid's bunker, which was built during the Blitz," said Cockney, "It was so deep you could pick lumps of coal out of the walls to shove on the fire to keep warm."

Cockney's real name was Colin. He and his family had moved up north from the east end of London, so we called him Cockney because of his villainous accent. Poor Cockney was at a dreadful disadvantage when it came to girls. We all felt really bad for him. He had been cursed with long, dark, shiny hair, parted just off-centre, an aquiline nose, piercing blue eyes, high cheekbones, a dazzling white smile, and athletic frame, and a sparkling personality. This had sadly made him altogether too conspicuous. They unashamedly smiled at him and brazenly attempted to sit next to him at lunch and incessantly sent him notes by the bagful. It really was too bad because he was such a nice lad, and to be afflicted that way was tragic. He was, of course, always treading on dangerous ground; it was something that would plague him for the rest of his life and put him in a very precarious and unenviable position regarding our gang rules. He would bemoan his terrible plight, often wishing he could be like Pugsley.

We all admired and envied Raymond Pugsley. He never had any of the kind of issues Cockney had. Girls and dogs avoided him at all costs, babies cried when he smiled, and old people paid him money to leave restaurants. We always sent Pugs into our den first, in order to scare any rodents out before the rest of us piled in. Yes, when it came to girls, Raymond Pugsley had been blessed from birth with natural and enviable immunity.

Cockney said that his family's move north had all been a bit sudden, after his dad had to go to court one day and give a speech to the judge about a group of men. These men were all from the east end of London, wore dark suits and very thin ties, and sat on a big wooden bench between two police officers. He said that living in the north had a peculiar effect on his family, for since moving here, his dad had taken to dying his hair blond, wearing a false moustache and sunglasses all the time, even at night. He also spent a lot of time looking underneath his car.

One thing we all agreed on when it came to a nuclear attack was that the least safe place was under our desks, as we had been told. What a way to go; the last thing you would ever see was 36 pre-pubescent backsides stuck in the air as you prepared to leave this world in the same position as when you arrived. The one thing we would have in the event of World War three was plenty of warning, as our school had been designated the centre of early warning for our district.

This was 1967, and technology being what it was, our early warning system consisted of an enormous great siren! Every week at our school, they sounded the siren, which was incredibly loud as it had been wired up to an amplifier and an exceptionally large bullhorn speaker. All of this was mounted on a platform six feet above the bushes at the end of our playground. It was so loud that we were warned when it would be sounded so we could cover our ears or stick our heads in the fire buckets. It was itself like a nuclear bomb; you did not want to be within a five-mile radius without taking certain precautions when it went off. This event occurred for two minutes every Friday during playtime, which was exactly 10:00 A.M.

Looking back now and understanding the Cold War, the siren at the south end of our school playground indicated that we would have only four minutes to live if it ever sounded in earnest. The siren's noise was so loud and obnoxious that, ironically, the only thought going through your head as you waited for those missiles to arrive would be, 'I hope they get here soon.' As ever, we had invented a game we liked to play, and like all our games, it was not fun unless it elicited the possibility of losing either life or limb. Blaster was such a game.

To participate in Blaster, you had to climb up on the platform and stand as close as you could to the siren for as long as you could while you were timed. The record holder was Whatty Jones, who had managed six seconds on the platform before having to jump into the bushes below. He then spent the rest of the day in class yelling "What!?" at the teachers at the top of his voice and pulling pieces of privet out of his undergarments. Thus, his nickname 'Whatty.'

Being a new boy, Leonard Farris wanted to impress us and go for the record. This fateful decision led to several calamitous events. The scene was set. On Friday, September 13th, at 10:00 A.M, Leonard Farris attempted to make history. Unknown to us, Farris had devised a devious plan, which some in our gang later judged as ethically questionable.

That morning at 9:59 A.M., as he made his way up onto the platform, we did not know that he had decided to use earplugs to beat the record. Not real earplugs, that would have been far too sane and sensible. No, unable to find any real earplugs, he had improvised, a decision that would have catastrophic results for us all. In the absence of real earplugs, he had decided to use peanuts; whole peanuts shoved deep into both ears. We should have known something was wrong earlier that fateful morning when he kept shouting "Yes" to us and nodding vigorously no matter what was said.

"Are you ok, Lenny?"

"Yes!"

"Are you ready, Lenny?"

"Yes!"

"Are you an idiot, Lenny?" He would nod vigorously, yelling,

"Yes!"

He trashed the record, setting one that no living mortal will ever surpass. He became the Bob Beamon of Blaster, standing there waving at us for a full twenty seconds. We were all suitably impressed and carried him shoulder-high around the playground, cheering, until Teddy Fothergill tripped and fell, taking the rest of us with him. Poor Lenny ended up being thrown into the bushes and spent the rest of the day in class shouting "WHAT?" at the teachers and pulling pieces of privet from his underwear—an inglorious end to a glorious feat.

Sadly, that was not the end of things. When the teachers discovered the nuts shoved into his ears, his parents were called for. Our game was exposed, and we were all asked none too politely to present ourselves before Mugger Murdoch in the Headmaster's study. We called him 'Mugger' because of his ability to seize you by the neck, wring a confession out of you, give you a thrashing, and have you walking down the corridor back to class in less than thirty seconds. His study was like the Bat Cave: large, dark, cold, and forbidding. He was kind of cool, in a dysfunctional superhero sort of way. He did not so much arrive as appear in our midst. There was a swoosh of his cape, and there he was, with mortar board and cane like an old silent movie villain. He was tall, dark, and ominous, with a hooked nose and beady eyes that missed nothing and made you think he knew what you had done with your brother's present the previous Christmas. "Well?" he demanded. When I said that at home, my dad would say, "That's a very deep subject," and laugh, thinking he was funny. I decided that this was not a time for levity. Like my dad said after he was told of the incident, it was not our fault if a kid shoves peanuts down his ears. However, he went on, "The game was a game fit for idiots," gazing at me as he made the comment. Surprisingly, the Headmaster agreed with my dad and chewed us out for being stupid, which he said we came by honestly. I wondered if I should tell my dad what the Headmaster said about coming by stupid, honestly, but I thought better of it.

Old Mugger spared us a thrashing, and we thought that was that. It was not. The doctors had a heck of a time getting those peanuts out of Lenny's ears; in fact, they discussed the possibility of surgery. The following Monday, we all met at the playground under the big oak, which was our spot, when the girls were playing rounders, and we couldn't go behind the bike sheds.

After we had asked Lenny what the doctors were going to do for the fifth time, he answered us very loudly, producing a bottle containing a thick orange substance from his satchel, at which we all shuddered instinctively. "No surgery!" he yelled; we all nodded our understanding. "The doctor gave me this, three times a day," he shouted, holding up three fingers. We grimaced but nodded. We passed the bottle around, studying the strange orange brew. Big George tapped Lenny's shoulder and pointed to where his dad was waving. Lenny then ran over to see what his dad wanted. "Poor Len," said Beaky, "having to take this."

"I wonder what it tastes like," said Mikey. Topsy suggested someone should taste it. We looked around. No one spoke, then Ginger said, "Give it here." He screwed the top off and tasted the vile-looking concoction. His face froze, his eyes dilated, and he made a high-pitched whining noise before doubling over and using the word usually reserved for when trapping your fingers in the car door, or when Bolton Wanderers were scored upon, which meant we all swore a lot on Saturday afternoons. Ginger was fearless; he was our school goalkeeper, and like all goalkeepers he was a bob or two short of a full piggy bank. However, he was also very agile, and the combination of agility and stupidity should never be underestimated. It came in useful more than once.

Of course, everyone had to try it after Ginger took a sip. So, we passed the bottle around, each of us taking a sip and reacting like Ginger, except for Wolfy. There was almost a glimmer of enjoyment in his eyes. We were all coughing, hacking, choking, and cussing when Limpy started laughing, which made us all hack and cough whilst laughing hysterically. The laughter was partly because it tasted so bad, but mostly because Lenny had to down this stuff three times a day, making us laugh even more. Lenny returned and asked why we were laughing, but we did not tell him. "What did your dad want?" I asked.

"To remember my medicine," he said, and we laughed again.

"Take it now," said Beaky through his tears; we all wanted to see this.

"Ok," he said. We could hardly contain ourselves. He opened the bottle, tilted his head, poured the medicine into his right ear, and then did the same into his left. "It dissolves stuff," he shouted. There was a stony silence as we all started hacking and spitting, but this time without laughter.

For the rest of that day, we were convinced that our time had come. It seemed we were all going to die of ear acid poison, which was a tragedy, as we were only nine. What would be our epitaph? 'He had just learned to tie his shoelaces.' We were determined to spend our last hours together, so we bunked off school, pooled our meagre resources, and went and bought fish and chips for ten, accompanied by multiple cans of Vimto and numerous Mars bars, Walnut Whips, and Curly Wurley's. Nothing mattered now, as we were all headed for that great football field in the sky, where girls were silent, dogs roamed free, brothers were optional, candy grew on trees, with thousands of bikes to ride and trees to climb, in an endless school-less summer that stretched way off into eternity.

We said goodbye sombrely as it would be the last time we would ever see each other in this world, and then we headed home. After an hour, I began to feel ill. This was it; the end had come at last. My whole life flashed before my eyes; it took four whole seconds. It was over before it had begun. Convinced these were my last moments, I fessed up to my mother, who laughed as she poured a large amount of Milk of Magnesia into a glass. I could not believe it; she laughed as her youngest and only human son was slipping into the next world. What kind of mother was she to find mirth in my imminent demise? She explained that I was not going to die, "Well, not right now," she said, "but maybe when your father finds out you skipped school," she shook her head. Skipping school was right up there with treason, murder, and playing football on the local bowling green. I called the other lads, who were also relieved until the realisation hit us that we would be back in the Bat Cave on Monday, and this time there would be no last-minute reprieve.

That is how the first week of school unfolded for us that year. Most people say that nuclear war is the scariest thing that can happen to anyone, but the people who say that have obviously never played 'Yeller,' a game of such astounding stupidity that it fair takes the breath away. In today's risk-averse world, the term 'putting it all on the line' is usually meant figuratively, but in 1967, it was never more terrifyingly literal, especially when a group of small boys discovered the concept of escalation. What happened on the rail tracks that day in October of 1967 remains etched in all our memories even to this day, especially for two boys—one who would stare into the abyss and the other who would become a legend.

October

Chapter 2
Neither First nor Last Be

———◆◦◆———

B y the end of the first week of October, having recovered from ear acid poisoning and a thrashing from our Headmaster, we were at it again, engaging ourselves in the game of 'Yeller.' As the world began to turn all shades of coppery red, gold and burnished bronze that Autumn of 1967, we found ourselves on the railway line at the back of our street.

Here a short disclaimer must be inserted as a token attempt to somehow mitigate the sheer and crass stupidity of what is to come. The brain of a nine-year-old is always developing. Some of that development comes at a much slower rate than others, which can often lead to thoughts, impulses, and actions that most sane adults would consider hazardous. Risk management for us in those days was watching some other kid fall off the slide. Hazardous was not a concept readily embraced even by adults in the late 1960s.

Smoking, for example, was considered healthy and good for frayed nerves, soothing anxiety, de-stressing, and the promotion of relaxing sleep. It had not yet occurred to my parent's generation that the sleep that cigarettes promoted was extremely long and involved a six-foot-deep hole and a wooden box. Nearly everyone smoked in those days, especially doctors, who ironically killed themselves by the thousands in an attempt to relax and get a better night's sleep. In fact, they even gave out Green Shield stamps to speed you on your journey to the great beyond, for with every pack of cigarettes purchased you received reams of stamps. Eventually, after filling up five whole books full of stamps, you could then trade in five years of your life for a leather encased travelling clock. When my mother's friends came round to the house on Thursday nights, the living room would fill up with smoke to the point that the ladies, eyes watering and coughing continually, spent the night talking to people they could not see. Mrs. Travers from across the road sat there talking for twenty minutes before she realised everyone had gone home.

Apparently, we were all indestructible in those days, as there were no seatbelts, airbags, smoke detectors, Heimlich manoeuvres, or helmets. Sugar gave you energy, red meat gave you strength, ice cream was full of calcium, and tea kept Britain caffeinated at the rate of one hundred million cups a day. There were lead water pipes and asbestos lining. Still, best of all was the wide selection of pesticides available for healthy families to enjoy as they frolicked in the cooling mist on summer evenings, as they watched dad spray the garden with an assortment of biohazardous chemicals now only reserved for warfare.

Is it any wonder that we did crazy things, and they didn't come any crazier than the game of Yeller? Together, our gang's total IQ barely reached double figures. Consequently, our health teacher, Mr. Schmitt, whom we suspected had slipped out of the Fatherland by U-boat at the end of 1945, had expressed concerns about some of our activities. He and the Headmaster had been intent on breaking up our gang for some time but found this problematic. They soon came to realise that the extra tuition required, when added to all our detentions and mandatory extracurricular activities, would inevitably result in the school having to build a bunkhouse for us to sleep in while the school governors prepared the adoption papers.

So, they gave up on that idea. Instead, they made us do extra PE and yard work. Mr. Schmitt made us watch movies with titles such as 'Which Way is Poland?' and his favourite, 'How Not to Grow Up as a Schweinehund,' we watched that one a lot. The shortest one we watched, which we never got to finish, was one about a cage full of monkeys, which he informed us at the beginning we would all relate to quite easily. After five minutes, he suddenly yelled, leaped from his chair, and yanked the plug out of the projector when Wolfy asked loudly what the chimps were throwing at their keeper. We did not find out for a long time. After that, we just marched up and down the playground with the rest of the kids to old Bavarian folk songs, clapping in time to Mr. Schmitt's whistle and waving at his outstretched arm.

If our parents had had any idea what we were up to when not at home or in school, they would have needed much more therapy than they were already getting. Happily, while they were only too aware of our potential for endangerment, they were oblivious to how much we actually put ourselves in harm's way. At the back of our cul-de-sac was the Manchester to Liverpool rail line, complete with embankments, trees, a high-level crossing, streams, and, of course, very large steam trains. This was a boy's paradise. All the journal entries that mention the game of 'Yeller' are up to these entries lacking any kind of awareness to the danger involved until this incident, which really seemed to have a sobering effect on us all.

First, you got excited about putting pennies on the rail line and seeing the Queen's head expand to three times its size as those big old puffers rolled over them. Eventually, we got bored with that and started putting empty pop cans on the line to be crushed, which also became tiring. Next on the rails was your brother's retainer and his model cars. On it went until you placed everything but your dad's car on the line. It all became a bore until we eventually decided to put ourselves on the line, which, believe me, never got boring.

The game was called 'Yeller?' or, more realistically, 'Last up, first dead.' The aim of this demented game was that we all lay down on the railway line and waited for a very large, very heavy steam train to come chugging around the corner. The first one to get up and run for it before Wolfy shouted, "All up," was Yeller, and he had to suffer the dreaded consequence of his cowardice. Of course, we all prayed that Wolfy would not fall asleep, as that would result in him becoming the world's first pre-juvenile mass murderer and the rest of us a confusing mess of jumbled body parts. This would be highly perplexing for the police who would find ten corpses but no brains. The consequences did not bear thinking about for a nine-year-old who showed 'Yeller' in front of his mates. If you were first up, you had to do the 'Walk of Shame,' a humiliation that was often too hard to bear. This had in times past resulted in a boy's spirit being broken, ending in the young funk scurrying back to his mummy, who would console him and wipe his bubbling lips, never realising that her son would ever be able to raise his head again in the milk line at school.

Worst of all, if you were first up, you had to wear 'Old Yeller'. 'Old Yeller' was a heinous piece of clothing. It was a yellow sweater, or at least it used to be, it was hard to tell anymore. Wolfy had found 'Old Yeller' in a very dark corner under an old bridge somewhere unspeakable. It looked like it had been the former residence of a family of hedgehogs that had littered continually in it for many years. It was rancid, slimy, and foul beyond description and had to be held at the end of a six-foot stick lest anyone succumb to the vilest stench imaginable. We had once carried it on a long pole to show it to Beaky's dad at his house, but chaos erupted when his dad started gagging, his mother passed out, and his pet skunk Orville tried to mate with it.

Wolfy said he remembered a kid at school a couple of years back called Oswald, who always wore a yellow sweater. He was the kind of kid who always did his homework, combed his hair, and washed his neck without even the merest threat of infanticide. This boy's mother had made him wear the sweater to school almost daily, which had been the last straw. In a fit of demented melancholia, Wolfy went on, warming to his story; Oswald had shinned down the drainpipe one night, slid down the embankment, and jumped a train for Liverpool in a bid to end it all by throwing himself into the River Mersey. We all winced. We knew that was impossible because our dads had told us that no living mortal who was not of Liverpool-born, could get within fifty yards of the River Mersey without a heavy-duty hazmat suit. According to Wolfy, Ozzy had discarded the odious yellow sweater as he boarded the train as a last act of de-fiance, leaving the life of a teacher-pleasing swot-obsessed oily tick behind him by allowing the eight-thirty-five from Piccadilly to whisk him off to another life. Wolfy believed that this was his sweater, recovered after all these years.

We had all decided that the offending garment was suf-ficiently nauseating to warrant its purpose. The one who turned Yeller, that is, the one who got up first from the track before anyone else, must wear this garment. He must then wade along the high-level stream that ran through a very dark tunnel under the railway tracks. Just gazing into that unfathomable darkness was enough to make the bravest shudder, for none knew, but all suspected what evil lurked in that black abyss.

Billingsley declared authoritatively that he had once seen a rat the size of a cat vanishing into the gloom of the tunnel at twilight with what looked like a small poodle in its mouth. Our belief that there were fouler things than rats under there, only served to confirm it as a fitting punishment for any such yellow-belly chicken to redeem his boyhood. The craven must wear 'Old Yeller' and bravely disappear into the unknown darkness of that black and haunted tunnel.

Having waded through the waist-high water and impenetrable darkness of the tunnel while wearing 'Old Yeller,' the 'chicken' was then pelted with gobs of mud by the rest of us as he tried to climb the slimy bank and extricate himself from both the stream and the sweater. Having done this, he would then be restored back into the ranks with full benefits. However, some struggled to climb the slippery slope. One poor boy only just made it out in time for his tenth birthday, but most usually just missed dinner.

It was clear to all self-respecting nine-year-olds that death was preferable to getting up first when that train came around the bend. Many kids never recovered from its shame and humiliation, let alone the scorn that was heaped upon them, along with the all-consuming mockery and derision. Worst of all, Cynthia Hardcastle, a goddess amongst other lesser girls, would hear about how craven you were, and that would be even worse than having to share your bed with your brother after a curry dinner and a box of After Eight Mints. So, on a cold and cloudless October day in 1967, we gathered on the railway line for what would become a day of unimaginable fear for one boy and turn another into a legend.

The ten forty-one was due. Billingsley put his ear to the track and declared it was coming. We were all impressed until we noticed the smoke billowing above the trees at the bend. Billingsley was still arguing that he heard the train before the smoke was visible as we lay down on the tracks. All the gang were present, plus Talky Tattersall, who was called Talky because he never shut up. He talked continuously, which was a problem at school as we were always being told to be quiet. It was rumoured that he was in the Guinness Book of World Records for the most detentions by a pupil in one calendar year. On one occasion, there were so many detentions that he did not go home for three weeks. His mother sent him his jammies and daily sandwiches. He was there so much that he began to call old man Balinsky, the school caretaker, dad, which caused a few raised eyebrows. A teacher had once commanded him to sit in the book closet and do his work; even then, he could still be heard talking. His brother Harold said he even talked in his sleep.

We all lay down on the line. We could hear and see the train getting nearer. This was the moment when you really pondered, as much as you could at nine years of age, about the true nature of existence and the real priorities of life. It is remarkable how you can gain a balanced perspective in these heightened moments. A sort of profound clarity comes over you as you lie there, rethinking your life. How bad could it be to be known as a craven coward, reduced to begging in the lunch queue, being despised by Cynthia Hardcastle, and being treated with contempt by all of humanity for the rest of your short life? It is at that moment when you think of your lifeless body being carried home to a distraught family and a smirking brother that you hear the words, "All up!" Then you scramble up off the tracks and fling yourself into the ditch at the side of the rail lines.

On that particular day, though, not everything went according to plan. Safe in the ditch, we turned to see one of the scariest sights we had ever seen. Limpy's sweater had snagged on one of the pillar bolts, and pull as he might, it would not release. Limpy was a slight lad with dark, greasy hair, that looked like it had been painted on his scalp. His name, considering there was no political correctness in those days, came from an accident he had that involved a non-too-bright older brother, a bottle of his Aunt Florence's elderberry wine, and an antique wolf trap that nobody thought still worked. Consequently, Limpy, despite having a perfect set of bubble gum playing cards of every division one footballer, was unfortunately not the most mobile of kids. The train whistle blew, and peering through the white smoke, the old shunter was now only forty yards away, with no chance of stopping.

We were all frozen with fright, for tug as he might, the sweater was not for giving. I will always remember the look on his face when he realised he could not pull it free. At the same time, the rest of us were frozen with terror; Talky was already on his way to Limpy. He had sprung into action, jumping the ditch and sprinting to the side of the track. He grabbed Limpy's sweater at the base and yanked it over his head, twirling him away from the track just in time to see the train clatter over the empty sweater. It was, as Limpy would recall over and again in the years to come, "A freakin' big train." Talky became an honorary life member of our gang. He even got a kiss from Cynthia Hardcastle. It was reported he did not wash his right cheek until he was thirteen.

That episode and the transition from steam engines to diesel trains enabled us to realise that we really were as stupid as most people said we were. We did not allow for the speed of the diesel trains, which were infinitely faster than steam trains and consequently incredibly more dangerous. On the last occasion, we played Yeller, we knew once, and for all, that, the gig was up because when that diesel flyer came screaming around the corner, we only just managed to get off the track. It was then that we decided to call it time on the game of Yeller.

I will never forget the look on the train driver's face as we clambered off the track. He looked like a man who had inadvertently relieved himself on an electric fence: his hair stood straight up, his skin stretched tight across his pale and waxy face, his eyes bulged while his mouth contorted grotesquely; he later found fame as British Rail's first and only living gargoyle. He looked for a moment like those many unfortunates who accidentally stumble into a Willy Nelson concert and cannot find the exit. The rest of us, on the other hand despite breathing very hard and no longer having any blood above the neck, were hoping there was at least one fresh pair of underwear in our bedroom drawer. Shaking and emitting high-pitched wheezing noises, like the cry of an arctic seal giving birth, it was a few minutes before we collected ourselves, grunted at each other with a sort of pre-juvenile masculinity, and decided it was time for lunch.

Of course, there would be many other times when life and limb were put at risk, but never again on the railway line. In time, the Manchester to Liverpool line would close, and by the end of the decade, all the tracks were gone, and it became a walking path. The only danger then lay in being run over by women with prams and the odd absent-minded bicyclist.

It would not be the last time that Talky showed great courage. Two years later, his family moved to the United

States, where he became a citizen. He later served with the Second Ranger Battalion in Desert Storm, operating behind enemy lines, where his bravery and quick thinking earned him a Silver Star.

Talky and I met one hot July day in San Antonio, Texas, a few years back. We sat in the shade of a sweet, scented lemon tree on San Antonio's famous River Walk, and over a cold beer, we talked about what happened on the railway tracks that day in October, almost fifty years ago. He had not changed a bit; as you can well imagine, he did most of the talking.

The dark, leafless trees and cold winds of late October marked the turning of the year. The clocks on the mantle were taken down and turned back. The curtains were drawn earlier, and the slate grey days began to draw in before the long winter nights. The last two weeks of October 1967 were spent, as they were every year at that time, collecting wood for Bonfire Night, which was just around the corner. Bundled up against the autumn chill, we headed out into the neighbourhood in search of wood. We would do anything to get wood for our bonfire. We were willing to face any challenge and surmount any difficulty or obstacle presented to us, natural or not.

November

Chapter 3
Bonfire Night

H aving survived the threat of nuclear attack, ear acid poisoning, and a ten-ton steam train, you would have thought there was nothing left to fear. But as Gandalf the Grey once said, "There are fouler things than nuclear missiles and locomotives in the world." Well, he probably didn't say that, but he should have, for that November would have proved him right.

England is never more beautiful than in the Autumn. The leaves of late October, having turned to orange and gold, had begun to float idly down beneath a pale and watery sun. It was a time when the air was full of pine scent and wood smoke. The damp leaves gathered on the cold pavement, and the wind carried a distinct chill that reminded us that winter was not far away.

Nothing in the journal seemed more evocative of those far-off days than the entry describing bonfire night. The entry revealed a detailed record of just how and where we collected our wood and all that it entailed. Sometimes, you are called upon to do things in life that are above and beyond the call of duty. One such occasion was Bonfire Night, November 5th, 1967. The day commemorates the capture of Guy Fawkes, who had tried to blow up the Houses of Parliament. Apparently, many people have dreamed of doing this through the centuries, not least my dad, especially when Harold Wilson won the general election and became Prime Minister of Britain three years earlier. Every neighbourhood had its own bonfire, on areas of open ground within each individual community.

This could be problematic as one bonfire built on some wasteland not far from our area got out of control and burned the fire station down, which was directly adjacent to the bonfire plot. Everything went up in flames, including the two brand new fire engines that would, under normal circumstances, have been called to come and put the raging inferno out had they not themselves been approaching seventy-two thousand degrees centigrade at the time. Eventually, bonfires would become regulated, but until then, it was bonfires galore. So, they continued to pop up everywhere in the Autumn of 1967 as November 5th grew closer.

Our job as kids was to collect as much wood as possible from wherever we could get it and build our community bonfire. This consumed our tiny little minds for weeks before the big night. We left no stone unturned, and no piece of wood was safe if it wasn't nailed down. We had to have the biggest and best bonfire in the area at all costs. Those weeks in the Autumn could be precarious for local residents, for if you weren't vigilant and careful, your front gate and garden shed could disappear in the night, only to turn up nestling at the foot of some bonfire somewhere. Often, red-faced men with angry looks, uttering words that no nine-year-old should hear, would be seen carrying their gazebos back down the street, having rescued them from a fiery end.

It was not uncommon in those days for a group of boys who grew up together in the same neighbourhood to refer to themselves as a gang and even have certain rules and regulations. These were benign childhood gangs that had no malicious intent, not like the gangs of today. Unlike the gangs of today, we couldn't drive, and under no circumstances were we allowed automatic weapons, or weapons of any kind, especially after the unfortunate incident with Billy Jenkins grandad's service revolver from World War One. Billy somehow smuggled it out of the house, and we took it on the railway line to shoot cans, or so we thought.

The gun was big and heavy; it took two of us to hold it and three of us to pull the trigger. We set up the cans, but with five of us working the gun, our aim wasn't exactly steady or even remotely close to the direction of the cans. In fact, most of the time, the muzzle was aimed at two lonely clouds drifting away from us as fast as they could. I had seen aiming like this once before when a very nervous contestant was trying to win ten thousand pounds on an episode of the Golden Shot TV show one Sunday afternoon. The contestant was shaking uncontrollably and consequently failed to hit the target, narrowly missing Bob Monkhouse and nearly killing Bernie the bolt with his own weapon. Eventually, after lots of pushing and shoving and shouting and swearing, we did manage to pull the trigger, but to our disappointment, the old revolver just clicked quietly; it was all very anticlimactic. There were no bullets in the gun. Already foreseeing such eventualities, old man Jenkins had removed all the ammunition.

There were ominous signs of things to come, though, like one evening as we were collecting wood from another local bonfire that had been foolishly left unguarded. A kid from another neighbourhood rode past on his drop-handled five-speed racer and launched an apple at us, which hit Foggy Holdsworth on the back of the head. I believe that it was the first drive-by fruiting in our neighbourhood, a sign of terrible things to come.

So it was that we toiled long and hard beneath blue October skies that turned red and gold at the end of each day, signalling the yellow streetlights to flicker into life and call time on our daily efforts. It was the universal signal to all boys everywhere in those days to head home. Over the next few days, we canvassed the entire area of our neighbourhood for wood. We knocked on every door, but it was hard to come by that Autumn. Our anaemic-looking stack of wood looked more like a half-built teepee than a full-blown bonfire. Something had to be done. Billingsley called for a council of war at our old den on the railway embankment.

So, we retired to the den. The den was our hideout on the old railway line. We had dug deep into the side of the railway embankment and shored it up with old pieces of corrugated iron and discarded railway sleepers so that we could all sit inside. It was precarious, to say the least. We were all one good sneeze away from being buried alive. It was used for meetings and deliberations. Deliberations were solemn events, usually held when a judicial inquiry was launched, like when Limpy had been seen holding hands with a girl. He was subsequently acquitted since the only witness was Wall-eyed Mike, who testified that four blurry characters, looking suspiciously like Limpy, seemed to be fraternising with what appeared to be a large house plant but could have been a girl.

The case was thrown out on the grounds of insufficient evidence. Had he been found guilty, the sentence could have ranged from being placed on probation and fined three packets of Beech-Nut chewing gum to suspension or banishment. The most severe punishment other than banishment was being forced to sit in a room and listen to Simon and Garfunkel records. However, this was stopped after Beaky read an article in Boys Own in which Amnesty International had outlawed this as a possible crime against humanity.

Beaky was the real brains of the outfit; we called him Beaky because he was small and round and had two large tufts of hair that stuck straight up on either side of his head. This, combined with a hooked nose, on which perched a pair of huge round spectacles, gave him the appearance of a constipated owl. However, he had scored a D- on every maths test that term, which was at least three grades higher than the rest of us. Mr. Nutall, our maths teacher, had once glowed with approbation about Beaky, declaring him, without doubt, the least stupid of the entire gang. Rare praise indeed from the Nutter!

At this time, Wolfy reluctantly informed us that his favourite uncle's first cousin's best friend had received a call to come to remove some old wood from a house here in our area. We were all very excited at the news and inquired of Wolfy which house it was. He stammered and said his favourite uncle's first cousin's best friend had refused to go, so he knew it was still there. We asked again, and again Wolfy demurred; something was amok. It is the kind of suspicious feeling you get when your mother serves what she tells you is fish, but it looks and tastes a lot like tripe.

Wolfy was my best friend. I had known him for as long as I could remember. For years, when I looked at Wolfy, I tried to work out just what it was about him that was missing after I had overheard Miss Winstanley, the school nurse, whisper to her aid that he wasn't all there. Wolfy was thin and wiry, with sandy hair, a long square face, and brown eyes that missed nothing. He was quite athletic and freakishly strong for his age. He was fearless, loyal, and possessed a wicked sense of humour. Best of all, he was always ready to do what no one else would or should. Mr. Fewkes, our Geography teacher, who had taught most of Wolfy's siblings over the years, had asked Wolfy, as we were filling out medical forms for a field trip to North Wales, if there was any history of sanity in his family. That said it all.

We continued to press Wolfy about the wood until he blurted out that it was at the Chambers' house. We all froze, eyes wide open, mouths ajar. Frothy, who had spittle issues, was bubbling wildly about the mouth. We all ducked for cover as he yelled the word, we were all thinking, "No!" Frothy lived just down the road from me. He was very tall and gangly for his age and had a kind of alien look as his was oval like a rugby ball. The loathsome seven-year-olds at school secretly referred to him as 'Martian head,' which was a bit low even for them. When he got excited, which seemed to happen with alarming frequency, spittle would form around his mouth, and if you weren't wearing your duffle coat or got your hood up when he yelled like he was about to, you were in for a good drenching. We all huddled in when the mist around Frothy's head had settled. "The Chambers' house?" we said in unrehearsed unison. The quiet undertone of resident horror was unmistakable. "No bonfire is worth that," said Ginger, studiously weighing up the possible consequences of a visit to the Chambers' house.

The Chambers' house was nestled in a small, wooded area at the bottom of the avenue. Behind its vast and forbidding wrought iron gates lay a winding path that everyone knew led you to your doom, or at least life in an unearthly altered state. There were three sisters who lived there, old spinsters, everyone, and recluses, who were only seen around town on blood moons and pension day. There was old Miss Chambers, who was the youngest of the sisters, then next in age was very old Miss Chambers, and then their even older sister, possibly dead Miss Chambers, she was called that because even though she was wheeled around in an old Victorian bath chair, nobody actually ever saw her move.

"It's a lot of wood," said Wolfy.

"How much wood?" Limpy asked suspiciously. Wolfy thought hard, possibly too hard, as his one lazy eye straightened for a second, then wandered back again. He raised a finger,

"A lot!" he said again.

"We could steal it," said Mike.

"No good," said Beaky, "bound to be cursed."

"True," we all mumbled in agreement. There was nothing for it; we would have to ask permission. Someone or two would have to pass through those iron gates and walk the path of no return.

"We will have to draw straws," I said, picking up a dozen twigs, two shorter than the others. Limpy went first and drew long. Beaky presumed by going next that he had less chance of drawing a short straw, and so it proved. Frothy was practically in a lather when he drew his straw," Yes!" he spurted all over Mikey, who had also drawn long. One by one, we drew with an air of increased foreboding now gripping our young hearts. Billingsley drew a long twig, stating he knew all along that he would, as the blood returned to his face, and he stopped shaking. Big George asked if there would be food involved and then drew when we said probably not. There were only two of us left: Wolfy and me. I hadn't the heart to burst his last glimmer of hope, so I let him pick, "Short!" he cried before realising that the little piece of twig in his hand might result in him spending the rest of his life as a frog. "It's you and me, old pal," I said, trying to remain calm while envisioning a myriad of unearthly consequences.

The next day, we met at the gates. It was one of those overcast but mild November days that marked the turning of the year. The last leaves of Autumn clung stubbornly to the trees; it was as good a day as any to be put into a stew. We hugged our comrades and gave them the letters that Wolfy and I had written to our mothers in case we were never seen again, telling them we loved them and were sorry for making them say our first and middle names so much. In the letter, I had also confessed to my brother what had really happened to his beloved goldfish, Jonathan and Maude, when I accidentally let Ripper, our pet cat, into his bedroom. I am sure that with names like that, they were glad to be eaten. It also recounted what happened to his favourite model, the seventy-eight-gun Man-o-War ship Indefatigable, the four-thousand-piece model he had painstakingly pieced together over two years. He had struggled for a long time to work out how it could have fallen off the shelf when it was secured on its plinth. The truth was that it couldn't withstand a single broadside from a cricket ball at five feet without shattering into a million pieces. It proved unworthy of the name. It was all there in black and white.

Off we went, through the iron gates and down the grey slate path beneath leafless trees and lifeless plants, like a scene from Grimm. We trekked until we spied the cottage. We could see movement through the kitchen window, and smoke belched out of the chimney; it was like the opening scene of Macbeth. I was scanning the skies for low-flying broomsticks and wondering what life might be like as a spider when we were spotted. A shrieking wail pierced the grey afternoon, "What are you two boys doing?" it asked.

"Nothing," I yelled. It was the stock-in-trade reply when any adult, especially parents, asked that.

"Come here at once!" she barked. It was old Miss Chambers. "Don't skulk, boy," she chastised, "and stand up straight when you're being spoken to." I wondered if she was related to my mother in some way.

"What do you want? Speak up! Well?" She folded her arms and glowered down at us over Pince Nez spectacles. She was ferocious, to be sure, but she didn't look like she ate small boys—well, not more than twice a year, and with luck, she might just have fed.

"We came for the wood," I spluttered.

"What wood?" she replied.

"The wood, wood for our bonfire," I persisted.

"The wood. Wood?" she repeated. "Oh, you mean the collapsed shed? Well, why didn't you say so?" she retorted. "Yes, we have wood. Come in the house for a minute, and you can bring your pet too if you like," she said, looking at Wolfy.

This was it; this was the moment when we would pass through that door and into their lair. The house would have a bubbling cauldron full of fish heads, lizard guts, and toad skins. Come to think of it, it wasn't really that different from what we were served at school every lunchtime. We went through the old dark doorway to what seemed like our certain doom. To our surprise, there was no cauldron, cobwebs, or deer skulls, just an ordinary house full of ordinary things. There was a table with a teapot and what looked like a delicious chocolate cake. At the table sat very old Miss Chambers, who exhausted herself raising a smile.

There, in the bath chair by the fire with a plate of cake in her lap, was possibly dead Miss Chambers. I watched for move-ment, but there wasn't any. "You boys need some cake?" said old Miss Chambers, "And some milk?" she continued. Were we to be poisoned after all? Were we being lured by nice old Miss Chambers into a sense of false security only to be seen off by a piece of poisoned gateau? If we were, it wasn't working because Wolfy had already finished his slice and was licking the plate, all with no ill effect. The milk and chocolate cake Miss Chambers gave us proved not only to be harmless but also delicious. As we left, I was mystified, as possibly dead Miss Chambers' plate was clean of chocolate cake, except for a few crumbs, and her teacup was empty, yet I never saw her move once. Very old Miss Chambers smiled once more and promptly fell back asleep.

Outside, old Miss Chambers showed us the wood. It was a goodly pile and well worth the risk. "Come tomorrow," she said, "Bring your friends, and you can take it away. What's more, moving it is worth half a crown to you all." Half a crown! That was ten Milky Way's two Walnut Whips and a Bar Six in our currency: a princely sum. Now to, find the gang and tell them. We had to chivvy them out of the den. They were pleased to see us, of course. We told them everything and were regaled as heroes for about half an hour or so.

I asked Beaky for our letters back, but he blanched and spluttered. This wasn't good, so I asked again.

"We thought you weren't coming back!" he cried. His words had something dark and ominous about them.

"We were only gone forty-five minutes," I yelled frantically, "Where are they?" I persisted, my voice rising at least two octaves.

"I gave it to your mother" he cried, as the full horror of what he had done gripped my young body. My whole life, what there was of it, flashed before my eyes. Even now, the opened letter would be lying on the table: my mother would be happy at the outpouring of my affection for her, my father absentmindedly indifferent, muttering something to the effect of, I knew that boy would come to a sticky end someday. It was my brother that scared the living Evian out of me. I could see him in my mind's eye; he would be staring into space, dreaming of all the things he would do to me, his gaze filled with pure malevolence. Whatever good there was left in him would have by now surrendered itself to the 'dark side'.

I thought of how my parents would feel with one son dead and another in jail for the rest of his life. I briefly thought about joining the circus; after all, according to most of my teachers, a red nose and oversized shoes would fit my personality perfectly. The foreign legion sounded more fun. I had read 'Beau Geste,' and the prospect of falling in battle in the desperate desert struggle against the Bedouin seemed very alluring at that moment, or even dying heroically in the black hole of Calcutta was more appealing than what my brother had in mind.

I thought about not going home at all, but I couldn't just not show up; I mean, they would notice eventually. Although, one of my greatest fears had always been getting trapped in the coal shed at the bottom of our garden in the summer when no one ever went there. You would never be heard yelling due to its distance from the house. I used to imagine my family sat at breakfast and my dad saying, pity about our Jimmy, whatever became of him, how long has it been now five weeks?" In the end, I decided to risk it and returned home. Due to the letter, I had become the little darling of my mother and, as such, came under her protection, a protective power that even my 'Sith' of a brother could not contend with.

That Bonfire Night was the best ever! We had the biggest bonfire in the area, blazing long into the night. We asked Beaky's dad, who usually lit the bonfire (as we weren't allowed near petrol of any kind, ever since we tried to launch our home-made rocket ship in Limpy's backyard, which blew all our eyebrows off) if old Miss Chambers could put the torch to the bonfire in honour of all the wood she gave us. He agreed. So, on that cold early winter's evening, old Miss Chambers lit the fire, and we let off fireworks and ate hot potatoes, Parkin, and Treacle toffee until we couldn't move. It was a huge bonfire that roared late into a now so-distant November night many years ago. I did not know it then, but it would not be the biggest fire I would witness that November.

Chapter 4
Dib Dib Dib

It was mid-November 1967. Bonfire Night was over, but school, which never ever seemed to be over, just went on and on. I remember that day because it happened during Arithmetic class. I was busy staring out of the window as usual when Wolfy bounced into the chair next to me. Cynthia Hardcastle had just walked past my desk, and Miss Collingwood, my teacher, told me to put my tongue back in my mouth and to continue exploring the possibility that six plus seven might add up to something other than eleven.

Wolfy was even weirder than usual. He placed his satchel between us and gave me a knowing wink with his good eye. "Sam," he whispered, "Sam is here."

"Sam who?" I whispered back.

"Sam, my cat," he said, looking down at his satchel.

"You brought Sam to maths class?" I said incredulously, whilst wondering what awful thing Sam must have done to be forced to come to maths class. People have it all wrong when they say that childhood passes quickly, but it doesn't; it is a myth. Anyone who has sat in maths class will tell you that not only does time slow down, but there are times when it actually stops, and hangs there forever, like your pencil as you decide where to put the decimal point. There are other times, too, when time slows to an agonising crawl like anytime my father sings, or Sunday afternoons visiting my aunts with my mother, or the one-hour TV show Panorama, the last one I watched lasted at least three weeks. Also, the last few days before school holidays, Christmas, or birthdays were always interminably slow. No, to be honest, it is adulthood not childhood that passes in a twinkling.

Wolfy did not answer. Instead, he opened his school bag a little, and sure enough, there was Sam, Wolfy's orange tom, staring back with a frightened look, just like the rest of us when we had to go to maths class. "What is he doing here?" I asked,

"My sister made me bring him," he hissed.

"Why is he having difficulty with his long division," I inquired. Wolfy's sister Carlotta was seventeen and was finally being allowed out at night again and had recently snared another unsuspecting youth to be her boyfriend.

His name was Alvin, and they had secretly arranged to meet at her house. The problem was that Alvin was allergic to cats. Apparently, on his last visit, Sam had caused Alvin to break out in hives and made his face to swell up so badly that he had frightened the postman, who had then called for backup from the village and a hundred people with pitchforks and torches had descended upon number 73 Doberman Street, yelling, "Kill the Beast!"

"You can't keep him in your bag all day," I said. "He needs to get out, plus he needs milk," I added knowingly.

"We can put him in the janitor's room at playtime," Wolfy suggested.

"Won't old man Balinsky notice he has a cat in his room?" I replied, but just as Wolfy was about to respond, Sam let out a low, deep yowl.

Two things happened at that moment: firstly, the whole class fell immediately silent, and next, the whole class looked at Big George. Big George sat at a desk on his own at the back of the class. George was a legend in his own lunchtime, a throwback to the days when there were no nutrition or obesity charts, no diets or exercise regimens. It was a time when every boy was expected to have a very healthy appetite. He had once downed twelve fish fingers, four helpings of mashed potato, and two portions of beans, after which he demolished three platefuls of jam tart and custard, all in one sitting. He was a force to be reckoned with. It was advisable not to get in his way when the bell went at snack time.

On one occasion, the school dinner van broke down and could not deliver any food. Tiny Teddy Fothergill was a very small boy in our class, so small that from the front, you could not see him for the desk. He had to raise a blue flag and wave it if he wanted to answer a question; it was a red one if he needed to use the little boy's room. On that fateful day, the dinner truck had failed to show up for school and everyone was very hungry. Big George was beside himself; there was an ugly rumour going around at the time that George had cornered Teddy in the cloakroom shortly after art class and eaten him. It turned out Teddy was at the dentist, so it all ended well.

"It wasn't me," George stated defiantly, staring everyone in the class down, "It wasn't." This time there was more of a tone of appeal in his voice. The class settled back down, and the hubbub masked Sam's objection to spending his morning in the dark and confining recesses of Wolfy's school bag.

"We need to put him in the big drawer at the back of the class," I suggested urgently. "He will be okay in there, it's big," I added.

"That's the art drawer!" said Wolfy, suddenly alarmed.

"What's he going to do, paint a picture," I hissed back at him.

"You're right" Wolfy said, there seemed no other way. We got to the back of the class unobserved and deposited Sam the orange tom in the Art drawer. Even with all the paper, paint, and brushes there was still plenty of room, and Sam seemed fine until we closed the drawer and sat down.

There was just something about that drawer that Sam did not like. The now high-pitched yowling, along with the crashing noises at the back of the class, was gaining way too much attention. "That is definitely not me!" yelled George defiantly, who was now on his feet. We could only watch in resigned horror as Miss Collingwood systematically tracked down the cause of all the commotion.

Finally, she narrowed it down to the Art drawer, then she dispatched messengers to the four corners of the school until eventually Mr. Balinsky the Janitor, Mr. Murdoch the Headmaster, and Mr. Johnson the games master appeared to find out what was in the drawer. The drawer was opened and there sat Sam, the world's first multi-coloured cat, peering up at them suspiciously. He was covered in paint, mainly blue.

At first, there was much discussion as to what exactly Sam was, with the janitor, Mr. Balinsky, who was standing at the back brandishing a hockey stick, exclaiming that he had seen one of these once on the BBC show, *World of Wonder*, presented by David Attenborough. Eventually, the cream of higher education realised it was a cat covered in paint, and out came Sam, along with the truth.

Once more, we found ourselves in the Bat Cave, which was how we kids referred to the Headmaster's office. I visited my father a few months ago to celebrate his 96th birthday. "I spent more time in Mr. Murdoch's office than my own," my father declared ruefully as we reminisced. That afternoon, Wolfy and I, and both sets of parents, met with Miss Collingwood and Mr. Murdoch to see what could or should be done with us. Mr. Wolfy talked about his time in the army and that when there was a breach of discipline, the miscreants learned the error of their ways by cutting the entire sports field with nothing but scissors or cleaning the latrines with a toothbrush. I thought that rather unhygienic. He obviously had not been in the boys' toilets here at school, which would require more of a flamethrower to sanitise them than a toothbrush. The reasons for the state of the boys' bathrooms were an ongoing debate. Opinions expressed behind the bike sheds as to why seven-year-olds can't pee straight were as wide and varied as their aim.

My dad suggested we both get a damn good thrashing, "Didn't do me any harm," he continued, with an air of validity. My mother scowled at him from behind her horn-rimmed glasses. Miss Collingwood inquired kindly if the blue cat had recovered from its ordeal. "Blue cat!" my dad said out loud, "sounds like a jazz club", and went on to tell a story about a little place with a similar name he and his buddies frequented during the liberation of Brussels in 1945. It was there, apparently, that they had danced till dawn with some local girls. It was with this last phrase that his voice trailed off, and he realised the story had gone too far, way too far. My mother turned slowly to fix her withering gaze upon my father, who seemed to visibly shrink in size. Miss Collingwood continued, "I think any discipline needs to be productive and educational," she said staunchly.

"Did you have something in mind?" Mr. Murdoch inquired eagerly.

"Yes, they both have way more energy than common sense," she declared. "I think they should both join the Cubs; there is a pack at the end of Emlyn Street. "That should keep them out of mischief and teach them some useful skills," she said triumphantly, and that is how Wolfy and I came to join Pack 428. I did not know anything about the Cub Scouts. According to Billingsley, it was founded by a man called Enoch Baden Powell, who lived just south of Wolverhampton. It was established, he said, so that the great urban unwashed could learn some useful life skills, like tracking deer through the suburbs of Birmingham or building a huge fire in West Park, to guide those poor, sad, hopeless, and weary unfortunates home from Molineaux on foggy nights.

Of course, before we were forced to attend Pack 428, I was grounded for a month. Imagine: no football, no friends, no playing out - it was a nightmare, Not the recurring nightmare I had recently been having where Cynthia Hardcastle, is visiting our house and my dad holds out his hand and asks her to pull his finger. Not as bad as that, but bad enough.

I was banished to my room most of the time to contemplate the error of my ways and rethink my life. I felt like that chap we read about at school, the Count of Montecristo, who had been jailed like me for no apparent reason, except for helping a friend with his cat. The Count had been locked away for life on a large, lonely rock in the midst of the ocean with no civilisation for miles around, no people he could talk to, good food to eat, any type of entertainment, or the remote possibility of a happy future. Because this sounded so much like the Isle of Man, many have understandably assumed that this was where the Count was imprisoned, but I am assured that it was an island in the Mediterranean Sea. Every year on the anniversary of his incarceration, he was thrashed with rope ends. Only Bolton Wanderers were beaten more often and more severely than the Count. He simply had to escape. For two decades, he had tunnelled through solid rock with a spoon; this was something I was familiar with every time I tackled my mother's rice pudding.

It was not that my mother was a bad cook. It was just that she was a little forgetful at times and things would get left in the oven longer than they should, like the rice pudding whose specific gravity usually tripled during its long duration. This made both serving and eating it extremely problematic. I bent more spoons than Uri Geller on her desserts. The oven was not her friend. The upside was that we always knew that dinner was ready when the potatoes exploded.

In the end, the Count's long, arduous attempt to tunnel out ended tragically when he thought he had reached freedom only to discover he had ended up in another cell. I had thought about tunnelling out of my room like the Count or Steve McQueen in The Great Escape, but I gave up on the idea. The possibility of trying to tunnel out of the house for years with a piece of cutlery only to come up in my brother's bedroom was too horrific to contemplate. I did not even like going into his room under normal circumstances, except for when I was intent on permanently borrowing something. In fact, it was that very act that saved my bacon after serving only ten days of my forced internment.

I secured early parole when our radio broke on the eve of the test match, and my dad desperately needed a radio to listen to the match. My mother had once again banished my dad to the shed; according to him, it was for being too logical. I happened to have a transistor radio that had somehow come into my possession about a year earlier. My dad offered to commute my sentence if I lent the radio to him. My brother then came into the shed looking for something with which to corral his pet rat Whiskers, who had somehow gnawed his way out of his cage and was even now trying to scale the north face of our garbage can in an attempt to reach Nirvana.

My brother said the radio looked very much like the one that had disappeared from his room under sinister circumstances the year before while he was at crafts camp. He lamented how much he had missed listening to the shipping forecast. Then he began to wax lyrical about increased northerlies coming in around Cromarty and Dogger Bank, with harsh gales across German bight and icy blasts blowing up around the Trossachs, which, according to my dad's interjection, brought tears to the eyes of Scotsmen everywhere. "What about Caroline?" I asked him incredulously, amazed that he had not yet been inserted into the Guinness Book of World Records as the earth's dullest individual. "Who is she?" he asked derisively.

"Radio Caroline," I stated with exasperation. This was the station I had been listening to at night under the covers with my torch and my secret collection of Mars bars and Turkish delight, the confectionary version, not the other kind. It was at this moment I realised my dad was still in the room and that this might be the shortest commutation in history. He eyed me knowingly for a few moments as I held my breath, and then he turned on the cricket.

Just before we went to Cub Scouts for the first time, my cousin Tom came to visit before he left for university to study philosophy. He was very cool. Along with his O' and A' levels necessary for university, he had earned something else, something very useful; he had earned his Duke of Edinburgh gold award for outdoor pursuits. This was and still is a very prestigious national honour. Very few are awarded this medal for outstanding achievement in wilderness activities and Outward-Bound programs. He could do anything; he could make fire by rubbing two Boy Scouts together or live in a small tent on the side of a Scottish mountain for 22 days in the depths of winter with two other campers, subsisting entirely on Heinz baked beans, cabbage, broccoli, and tinned prunes. My dad said they would have made it a month, but one of them lit a match in the middle of the night, and the tent went up in a big blue flash. Luckily, mountain rescue, as well as most of Scotland, saw the explosion and climbed up to rescue them. Many years later, he led the British Arctic Norway expedition. For years now, he has made his living as a mountain guide for climbers in the French Alps. He also makes documentaries on remote areas of the world for the BBC.

A few years earlier, my brother had tried to join the Cubs but had become frightened when they used a cap gun to start the sack race. He had not been expecting it and had to be given lemon barley water and an aspirin and left to sit in a dimly lit room until he was himself again. The writing had been on the wall for some time for him. For weeks prior to his first meeting, he had been trying to memorise the Cub chant of "dib, dib, dib" and couldn't. He was a Cub Scout for twenty-six minutes.

So, it came to be that decked in matching green sweaters complete with pack insignia, yellow kerchiefs around our necks, and a small green cap, we set off for our first night with the pack. I had a very hard time convincing Wolfy that in the Cubs, it was a three-fingered salute and that if he continued to salute with two, we would not be in the Cubs very long. We arrived on our first night to the sound of sirens and an eerie red glow in the night sky. Wolfy and I looked at each other excitedly; boy, these guys knew how to build a bonfire, except that it was not a bonfire, well, not an intentional one. Apparently, the lesson on learning how to put out a fire had gotten entirely out of hand, and when the fire extinguisher failed to work, and the pack got a first-hand lesson from the local fire brigade on how to extinguish a roaring conflagration as the Scout hut burnt down.

It was a very sad sight to see our future pack members standing forlorn around the blazing edifice, trying to game-ly sing Kumbaya. Fortunately, no one was hurt, and the blaze ran its course, totally destroying the old wooden meeting hall. That was the end of Pack 428. For many years afterwards, the burned-out remains of the site could be seen by all who passed by until it was absorbed into the local golf course and became a short par three.

Wolfy and I were never officially Cub Scouts, although we came within ten minutes and about a hundred yards, which was about as close as anyone could get to the scout hut that night. The inquiry returned the verdict of accidental conflagration due to antiquated wiring and the gross mal-functioning of the fire prevention equipment, which had not been tested since the beginning of the Boer war.

So it was that on that far-off cold November day in the fall of 1967, our membership of the Cub Scouts ended before it began. In time, everything returned to normal, including Sam, the cat, who had by then ceased to be blue. The upside for Wolfy and me was that we could spend more time that November preparing for the upcoming annual rugby game against our implacable foe, the unscrupulous Ronald Marchbanks and his team.

December

Chapter 5
They Think it's all Over

It was intolerably cold that December. Still, we didn't let that deter us as we prepared to face Marchbank's team in our annual rugby match, which an unsuspecting villager once described as murder with rules. This was grudge rugby at its best and bloodiest. It was a game between village rivals whose vitriol for each other was unrivalled in any competition, especially rugby. This was only two weeks after the sad loss of the village Scout hut, and morale was at an all-time low and had to be restored. We had decided that a collection should be taken at the game in support of building a new Scout hut. The collection was taken up by a pack of despondent and slightly singed cubbies who walked around with a bucket accepting donations from the villagers. The description of the rugby game that winter is the longest entry in the journal and quite accurately reflects the extreme competition there was between the two groups of boys.

You could not swing a cat around (I am speaking figuratively, of course, as the R.S.P.C.A. had been known to visit a few houses in our area after cats with extra-long tails started to appear) in our village without hitting a celebrity. We had singers, artists, and sports personalities, including one England World Cup winner. I am compelled to interject the little-known but enormously significant fact that I was once Alan Ball's paperboy, ensuring he got his Daily

Express every morning. In some small way, I like to think that I contributed greatly to his emotional well-being, which in turn helped us have our only moment of glory on that beautiful late July day in 1966 when football actually did come home.

I remember kicking a ball around with him and his son on our village green one Sunday morning. He was such a gracious, kind, and generous man; superlatives that few of his opponents would use to describe him on the field, but nonetheless true. Our village boasted three England cricket Captains stretching back to World War One. Of all the celebs that frequented our village, our favourite and the most loved celebrity was our local butcher, Peter. As a former professional rugby player, coach, Challenge Cup winner, and England International, he stood head and shoulders above the rest, like a young Perseus.

For years, we would all cram into his butcher's shop to watch him take a cleaver to a piece of brisket, slicing and dicing like he used to do on the field. Big and burly with a flat nose, cauliflower ears, a curly mop of black hair, no neck, and an easy grin, he would chat to us while he minced his beef before showing us out the door when the old ladies arrived for their daily pieces of scrag end.

Ronald Marchbanks, on the other hand, was a particularly unpleasant individual. His sole delight in life was humiliating us any way he could.

He was also the leader of a particularly distasteful pack of kids. They were our implacable foes at everything but mainly sports. Their dark lord and leader, Marchbanks, was our nemesis. A tradition had arisen whereby we played his team at cricket, football, and rugby every year on our local village green to see which of our gangs would bask in the glory of being crowned village champions and who would have the letter L painted on their foreheads.

One year, we played British Bulldog but were forbidden from ever doing it again by our parents, local community leaders, the town council, and the Lord High Constable of Manchester after what started out as a less-than-friendly game turned very ugly indeed.

The Marchbank's crew were an insidious lot and would do anything to win. Marchbanks also had designs on Cynthia Hardcastle. Fortunately, Cynthia could see through his oily charms and smarmy ways. During conker season, Marchbanks purported an act of such infamy that it lives to this day as a reflection of his need to win at all costs and the despicable lengths that he would go to ensure victory.

As small boys, we took our conkers very seriously, as you do. We hardened them through various forms of boyhood alchemy, which invariably included many and varied concoctions and machinations that, even now, we are not at liberty to disclose in detail.

Once hardened, we drilled a hole through the conkers centre, threaded a string through it, and tied a knot so the resilient nut was ready for combat. It was a discipline that served everyone well in later life. These contests included boys taking turns swiping at each other's conkers until one cracked or obliterated entirely. Every victory won was attributed to your conker. So, if you won four contests, for example, it was a 'Fourer,' if seven, a 'Sevener,' and so on, ad infinitum.

To the utter infamy of his name, Marchbanks had revealed his conker, which he had aptly named the 'Destroyer of Worlds'. It had quickly become a 'Twenty-Twoer,' utterly eviscerating every opponent, leaving a trail of destruction in its path of such searing proportions that many a small boy had run home misty-eyed to his mother in need of quiet consolation.

Topsy Hallworth's 'Brown Bomber', a 'Twenty-Fourer,' had made Topsy a legend, having conquered all before him. Therefore, Ronald Marchbanks demanded a showdown. A 'once and for all,' 'no holds barred,' 'winner take all' grudge match between the 'Brown Bomber' and the 'Destroyer of all Worlds,' which he privately referred to as Oppenheimer's pet. The venue was behind the bike sheds on a Thursday lunchtime in late October, a date that would live in perfidy as the two titans clashed for ultimate supremacy.

Topsy said he was not nervous, but the fact that he kept hyperventilating into his cheese and onion crisp bag told another story. Marchbanks stood imperious and very confident. It was all over in two blows. Marchbanks was ecstatically cheering and waving his conker wildly while Topsy was stunned. He manfully tried to stop his bottom lip from quivering, especially as Cynthia Hardcastle had been given a special invitation to the bout. Usually, girls were not allowed behind the bike sheds, where, apparently, according to girl lore, there were all kinds of unnatural practices.

It was then that it happened. In his excitement, Marchbanks accidentally let go of the swinging conker. It flew through the air like Thor's hammer, catching Timothy Hall, better known as Dodger, which was ironic because the conker zinged him straight in the head, poleaxing the poor chap. Immediately, we knew something was stinkier than Wolfy's underwear, as no conker, no matter how hard, should do that much damage. A small lump was appearing above Dodger's eye as Beaky picked up Marchbanks' conker and tapped his finger on it. It soon became evident that Marchbanks had been lacquering his conkers with brown nail polish, burnt spice, to be precise. Apparently, he had fiendishly swiped the varnish from one of his human siblings. As no one had ever touched it, he had succeeded in fooling all present until now. Marchbanks stood unrepentant. After the British bulldog incident, a measured response was called for; we would seek revenge on the rugby field.

So, we prepared to play our annual rugby match against Marchbanks and his crew on our local village green. We had asked Peter, our international former rugby-playing butcher, if he would come out to a couple of practices and give us some tips, which, to our delight, he did. After about twenty minutes of watching us grunting and shunting, yelling, straining, and flying around in all directions, he stopped the practice and asked in a somewhat mystified tone what game we were actually playing because it was not any form of rugby he had ever seen. Billingsley's dad said the last time he had ever heard or seen anything quite as wildly frenetic and disturbing as that was the day Farmer Newton's live power line broke and fell upon his metal chicken coup.

Peter taught us as best he could how to pass, tackle, scrum, and kick until we vaguely resembled something to do with the game of rugby. He said he would be there the following Saturday to cheer us on and have a couple of steaks for all our black eyes.

There was only one thing left for us to do before the big game: spy on Marchbank's practice to see what nefarious tricks he had up his sleeve. We had heard from Jingo Shuttleworth's sister, who was sweet on a young lad called Walter, who played wing for Marchbank's team, that they were running a secret practice on Sunday afternoon up on the old running track. This was a doubly good break for us, for not only could we scout Marchbanks' team, but we could accidentally, on purpose, let slip who told us where they were practicing. Goodbye, Walter!

Wolfy and I set off to see what Marchbanks had up his sleeve. What we saw as we spied on them from the over-pass bridge on the East Lancashire Road was chilling. We were both perched on the top ledge of the bridge, which was a bit tricky and took much nerve and concentration. Any loss of balance would mean falling forty feet onto the railway tracks below, where we would likely get run over by the three fifty-three from Piccadilly to Lime Street station.

There were some risks worth taking. Plus, the honking of horns, squealing of tires, and yelling from nearly every car that passed by on the East Lancashire Road behind us didn't help our concentration. Adults should know how irresponsible it is to distract a couple of kids precariously perched on the top of a railway bridge, concentrating on not falling onto the railway tracks forty feet below.

We did have Beaky's binoculars, though they could have been better as he had obtained them from a Lucky Bag he had bought for a tanner. Even the limited binoculars worked well enough to reveal Marchbank's secret weapon; he had done it again. There, like a huge dot on the bright green horizon, stood Jumbo Butterworth. Jumbo was a very big boy for his age, roughly the size of Dartmoor. He was the son of a Yorkshire pie maker, and the lad had developed an addiction to his father's delicious creations. In fact, Old Man Butterworth could not work out why he was moving product in his shop at an alarming rate, but somehow his profit margin had stayed the same. He obviously had not equated Jumbo reaching the seven hundredth percentile in growth for a boy of his age with his stock anomaly.

All Marchbanks would have to do is get Jumbo the ball, and there would be no stopping him. He would wreak havoc, leaving a slew of young bodies strewn about the field on his way to the try line. We had all heard about what happened when he played British Bulldog at school one lunchtime. That was the day poor old Frosty Fosdyke had failed to see Jumbo coming. It was terrible; they had to bring the dogs on after the game to search for his remains. As it happened, Frosty had been scraped up by Miss. Winstanley the school nurse, who was passing by. She had taken him to the school office, where they kept the iron lung machine.

In the end, though, Jumbo had become a cult hero after thrashing Crescent Valley Junior School's Tug-of-War team on his own. Jumbo playing for Marchbanks was unbeliev-ably bad news. This would be the worst beating since my brother decided to repaint our car. Something had to be done, and it had to be done quickly. We called an emer-gency team meeting in Peter's shop as he minced his beef for the day, which was always cool to watch. "Give him a pie," said Peter, "if he's so fond of them, that might distract him."

"Won't work," said Mikey confidently, as he went on to tell us that he once saw Jumbo swim two lengths of our local swimming pool with a pie in one hand without it ever getting wet. Ultimately, it was not pies or great strategy or any of that malarkey that saved the day; our salvation was to come from a very unusual and unexpected place.

Paula Postlethwaite was eleven and lived in a large white house at the back of our house. In fact, our gardens were only divided by a large wooden fence. In her garden was a large wooden structure that looked more like a small cathedral than a kennel. In that small cathedral lived the world's largest dog, at least that is what my dad called him. Harth was a Welsh wolfhound of medieval proportions. He once found his way into our garden unobserved while my dad was planting his geraniums. My dad found himself standing eye-to-eye with the great beast while it drooled with anticipation, making its mind up whether to eat him or trample on his nasturtiums, which would have been equally as painful. My dad later told us after his fourth whiskey and was much steadier that, he had decided to stare the great hound down as he had with Hitler's Panzers at Normandy. He said his iron resolve in the face of great danger had seen him through again; he then went and had a lie-down.

The most flattering compliment that could be attributed to Paula Postlethwaite was irritating. Superior would also work, along with many other words, many of which we learned from Wolfy. Paula was very precocious and fear-less; she should not be messed with unless there was no alternative. She had short blond hair, a small nose, large green eyes, and a wicked penchant for revenge. Wolfy and Paula did not get along, so the battle was joined when we saw her feeding her horse apples in the field beyond the old railway line. Paula loved nothing more than to make all our lives miserable. "Hi Paula," I said, trying to be at least neighbourly. She sniffed derisively.

"This is my horse," she said haughtily.

"I can see the family resemblance," Wolfy said casually. Paula ignored him and looked at me.

"Is his parole officer with him?" she asked with disdain. "I don't want him near my horse if he hasn't had his shots," she added; "I hear distemper can be so difficult to deal with." Wolfy was about to lurch, so I had to physically restrain him while placating Paula at the same time." Where are you going?" she asked.

"Rugby practice," I said.

"Ronald says you are going to get annihilated," she stated with bored indifference. She was, of course, a good friend of Marchbanks, as they had fallen from the same tree.

"You?" I inquired politely,

"My friend Luella is coming over for the afternoon, "before we go to Shirley's party." Shirley Marbury's party was the social event of the year. If you were eleven and a girl, it should not, indeed, could not be missed. Rumour had it one girl had missed it the year before and had become a social pariah, shunned in the snack queue at school, dishonourably discharged from the girl guides, and disinvited from sleepovers and makeup parties. Her life was over, and she was not even twelve yet.

Later that afternoon, the guys were at my house, and we were in my dad's garden shed when Wolfy appeared. "Where have you been?" Mike asked.

"Afraid to come in," said Wolfy, pointing at the broomstick outside by the door. "I thought Paula was here." We all laughed; good old Wolfy.

"I wish we could get her good," said Limpy.

"Maybe we can," Wolfy said knowingly as we followed him out of the shed. He climbed up on the garage and gazed over the fence into Paula's Garden. Sure enough, there they were. It was early December, and though the sun shone, it was very cold. The girls were bundled up in coats and scarves and sat out in the garden on lawn chairs, catching whatever sun they could and chatting about whatever it was that girls chatted about. It was time to act. Frothy and Mike got the cricket wickets, and I got a pair of my Grandads old braces, while Beaky and Snowy filled the balloons with ice-cold water. This was going to be good. Wolfy spotted from the top of my dad's garage.

We drove the two cricket wickets into the grass until they were very firm, then we tied the braces to them and adjusted for tension. The girls were just on the other side of the six-foot fence that divided our properties, at most twenty-five yards away. We could all picture that first balloon full of icy water landing on them. We put a blue balloon in the braces, pulled back as far as we could, and then fired. The first flew straight over the two girls, the lawn, the patio, and through the Postlethwaite's open French windows. Wolfy swore. "Too much!" he announced. The second was too far left and landed harmlessly in the rhododendrons. The next one had range but no direction and disappeared into Harth's kennel, which prompted a low and menacing growl. We heard Paula tell Harth to be quiet. Then Paula's mother came out and asked if the dog had been under the dining room table in the last hour.

The next one, a green one, got all tangled up and shot out sideways into Old Man Fanshaw's backyard, where a high-pitched yowl told us that we had shocked the Evian out of the feral cats in the long grass. The next one, a bright yellow one, found its mark. The immensely satisfying screams of the girls sent us into fits of hysteria. Wolfy told us later that the ice-cold bomb had hit Luella square on and splattered Paula as well. Wolfy laughed so hard that he fell off the garage roof. They had coats on, so it didn't do that much damage, but still. We were still on the lawn laughing and celebrating when Paula appeared over the fence, hose in hand; there was no escape. The water hit us with all the venom of a fire hydrant forced through the best hose money could buy, with a triple nozzle attachment for extra force. She did not stop until we were all thoroughly soaked and freezing, and her revenge was satiated.

Paula and Luella peered over the fence, gloating at their victory, when Wolfy said, "Look what she's done to your dad's flowers." We all looked over to see the violence she had accidentally wrought on my dad's roses and hydrangeas. These were my dad's little darlings. "Oh dear," I said, "he is going to be mad." And he was. He loved those flowers more than his own children. We knew this because he used to say, "These are my real children; they don't cost me money or make me swear, or drink, or seek counselling."

Paula was no longer smirking. Instead, her smugness had been replaced by genuine fear. "Don't tell him it was me!" she said sincerely. "He'll tell my dad, and we'll be grounded from the party. Please?" she continued, her voice becoming more and more desperate. I was enjoying this far too much. It was then that I got the idea. After some negotiation, Paula finally and reluctantly agreed to our arrangement. The price of my silence was Jumbo Butterworth's heart.

The day of the game came. Marchbanks and his team strode onto the field with all the arrogance of a team that knew it had won before even a ball was kicked. Jumbo wolfed down the remains of a pork pie and ambled onto the field. My star player, Paula, was on the touchline along with Luella and Suzy Jordan. This was a clash of the Titans, Paula verses Jumbo. May the best girl win! All week, as per our agreement, for me taking the fall for the flowers and

Paula being able to attend the party, she had been making 'goo-goo eyes' at Jumbo. She had a very ugly name for our agreement, but then all is fair in love and rugby.

It had worked; Jumbo was completely twitter-pated! Paula had woven her girly wiles in a web of intoxication until Jumbo had fallen for the most irritating girl in five square miles. She had sent him notes and smiled at him; on one occasion during a game of Hide-and-Seek, she had held Jumbo's hand, resulting in him emerging at the end looking all bashful, with a red face, standing on one leg and grinning from ear-to-ear. We had to make him eat a lemon to get the smile off his face.

Come game day, he was completely smitten, and with Paula on the sideline, he was totally useless. All she had to do was wave at him, and he tilted his head to one side, blushed, and stood on one leg again. That is not what you want from your second row-forward. He missed everything. Marchbanks was so angry he nearly did himself a mischief, yelling at Jumbo. But Jumbo was so far down lover's lane that he would have needed a road atlas to find his way back.

My genius as a master planner had surpassed even my own usual brilliance. It was then, as I was basking in the glow of self-approbation, that it all went wrong. Paula had left the field with her friends to go to the local shop across the road.

In her absence, Jumbo refocused. He received the ball in the dying minutes and set off for our try line. Wolfy was on his back, Limpy around his left ankle, and Mike hanging on his right arm, but he was still going. It was my turn to pile on to him, but it was no good. The Boyzilla dragged five of us along with him as I scrambled to loosen the ball, but to no avail. Jumbo held onto it like it was the last almond slice in the shop. He and the rest of us went over the line; it was a try, and Marchbanks team led by two in the final three minutes.

We kicked off; the ball was picked up by Marchbanks, who passed it again to Jumbo, urging him in less than polite phrases to move his giant frame. We all piled on again, but to no avail; our fate seemed sealed. Then, destiny took a hand when Mr. Whippy, the ice cream man, played his all too familiar jingle. It sounded like the heavens had opened to Jumbo, and celestial voices of angelic delight had poured forth in glorious revelation. Jumbo suddenly stopped, propelling us all through the air into a collective heap on the turf. In so doing, he lost his grip on the ball. The knock-on resulted in a scrum down from which we retrieved the ball.

Marchbanks was furious and banished a sulky Jumbo back to the fullback position. The clock was ticking down, and we were losing by two points. Only a few seconds remained. Our situation was as desperate as the day we found Bazzer Barnes in the toilets at our local park; he didn't have a penny for the stall and was standing there doubled over, his face strained, his legs wrapped tightly around each other, whimpering pathetically as he desperately attempted to pick the lock with a wet piece of string.

It was now or never. Frothy recovered the ball. I could hear Peter shouting, "Kick it!" Frothy did just that, booting it way up field toward the opposition try line and a very lonely Jumbo. At that moment, a dozen boys from both teams set off in pursuit of the ball, which had rolled over the try line and stopped; first to it would win the game! There was pulling and tugging and tripping and pushing and tackling and rolling and beating and bruising as this moveable melee of scrambling boyhood tumbled over each other in a frantic attempt to reach a stationary object that sat perched on the grass waiting to be seized for the glory it would bestow. Jumbo was closest, but blessed with size and strength as he was, pace was not his friend.

It seemed as if at least half a dozen players arrived at the ball at the very same moment that Jumbo threw himself at it. It was a terrible site. A piled mound of human flesh massed upon each other: legs, arms, and heads protruding from unnatural positions and emitting unearthly noises. It was like some giant hideous alien multi-headed mutant spider gasping out its last choking breath in the hostile and rarefied atmosphere of Earth. Onion Charlie, our local greengrocer, who was refereeing the match, finally arrived and attempted to untangle the twisted mass of humanity by disengaging one boy at a time. Some were so hideously misshapen that they were never the same again. Chalky Hastings was so bent over that Boy Scouts kept helping him across the road for weeks to come. In just thirty fateful seconds, Figgy Underwood had become double-jointed in both arms and one leg. Eventually, Onion Charlie worked his way through the mass of body parts until beneath this sprawling pile of boys lay the last and giant form of Jumbo Butterworth.

Most of the crowd had now come onto the pitch thinking it was all over, just like during the World Cup final the year before when England had beaten Germany 4-2 at Wembley. The great irony on this occasion was that Kenneth Wolstenholme, who had commentated on that game for the BBC and had famously quoted at the end, 'Some people are on the pitch, they think it's all over, it is now' when Geoff Hurst scored England's fourth goal, was actually one of the people on the pitch, having been born our village and still having family there had come to watch the game.

It took all of us to lift Jumbo to his feet. It was only then we realised that beneath Jumbo was something that had at one time been human, well, almost human.

"That's Wolfy," cried Snowy! We all gasped!

"Are you sure?" said Frothy.

"Hard to say," Mike mumbled.

It was then that Wolfy groaned once and rolled over. His face was green with grass stains, and there was soil in both ears, and a huge dock leaf wedged up his nose, but that did not matter because there was a collective gasp as we all saw the ball for the first time in what we believed used to be his hand. Onion Charlie declared it both a try and the worst thing he had ever seen in his life. Then it dawned on us that we had won the game! We stood Wolfy up, returned his collar bones to their proper place, declared him a hero of the first water, and carried him off the field.

Peter told us it was the most extraordinary rugby game he had ever seen. Kenneth Wolstenholme said he had never seen anything like it in all his days, which delighted us all until we grew up and thought about that statement a little more deeply. Paula cheered, even though she had no idea what she was cheering for, and Marchbanks was furious at everyone, especially Jumbo, who had now trotted off to find Mr. Whippy. Wolfy has kept the ball to this day, and when I visit his office, where it stands deflated and a little worn on his filing cabinet. We often talk of how he survived those fateful seconds at the bottom of that pile. He winces even now at the thought of it.

In reflection, it is astonishing how much those early skirmishes on the village green formed and framed not only our love of sports but also our competitive nature. As the years passed and the standard of competition increased, we began to realise just how much of our character and on-field personality was created during those early days, when winning wasn't everything, and it was the love of the game which drove us to both participate and excel. The learning curve varies for us all, but the one constant that always remains true, even when all else is stripped away, there is the undisguised joy of innocence, which is always best reflected in fierce competition and stems from a simpler and more carefree time.

Only two weeks were left now until the Christmas holidays, and then we were done with school for two whole weeks. With our victory over Marchbanks still being celebrated my thoughts were turning from rugby back to football. I was hoping to find my heart's desire under the tree, and it wasn't Cynthia Hardcastle, well, not this year.

Chapter 6
Best Christmas Ever

C hristmas came that year with chill winds, crimson sunsets, and jet-black nights that were crystal clear and filled with stars. They were a vivid and poignant reminder that the season was upon us. The thought of Christmas brought a glow to the hearts of small boys everywhere. We had all but recovered from the trauma of our victorious rugby game against Marchbanks and his crew, but It was football that preoccupied my thoughts that Christmas. Bill Shankly, the manager of Liverpool, had said it best when commenting on the importance of football, declaring "that football was not a matter of life and death, it was much more important than that."

The Lisbon Lions of Glasgow Celtic had just won the European Cup the previous May, playing in their famous green and white hooped shirts. I liked Celtic and Tommy Gemmell in particular. He was a right-footed, marauding left fullback who scored for Celtic that night in Lisbon. Also, we were only eighteen months removed from England's epic World Cup win at Wembley the previous year. As nine-year-old boys, we lived for Saturday mornings and our weekly kick-about on the village green. The dread of school was forgotten, and we all chipped in from our weekly ill-gotten gains to buy a bag of sawdust with which we marked out the lines of the football pitch. We all helped out, 18 of us marking the pitch one handful of sawdust at a time. This was hardly slide-rule stuff; the lines were not exactly straight. The goal line was so bad that the ball could be halfway into the net and still not have crossed the line. One team would yell, "It was in!" And the other would yell, "Never was!" The only way of resolving the argument was to appeal to whoever was standing at the bus stop adjacent to the field watching our game.

In retrospect, I believe that these random citizens of our fair town waiting for the bus to Swinton that day were the forerunners of what came to be known as V.A.R. On this particular morning, there was just such a controversy, and we had to turn to the bus stop adjudicators. The man in the tan overcoat and trilby called a huddle with the tall, gaunt man with grey hair and the small rotund woman in the scarf and curlers. After prolonged deliberation, the man in the trilby declared that it was definitely in, which provoked a mixture of cheers and boos and some rather un-nine-year-old language. "Do you kiss your mother with that mouth?" the man in the trilby yelled as he produced his little black diary and demanded the name of the boy who had just inferred that the man in the trilby may not have known who his father was. Nevertheless, the bus stop VARs had spoken, the game was over, and we had won 19 – 18. Win or lose, it was of no real consequence because, on Saturday mornings, we simply lost ourselves in the beautiful game. The journal describes those Saturday games in great detail, revealing just how important and meaningful those mornings on the green each Saturday really were to us all.

That Christmas, I had my heart set on a football, which may not be very ambitious, but this was not just any old football. It would revolutionise our game and would save those few of us who had one from future brain damage, as the ball was covered in plastic. It was important because that plastic coating made the ball waterproof. The old leather footballs that we played with were practically lethal. They were okay at first, until it got wet and gained a hundred pounds, in which case it turned into something more akin to a cannonball. The old balls had cross-stitched lacing on the outside, God forbid you had to head it when it was wet as it usually resulted in the premature fusing of every vertebra in your young body, temporary amnesia would then set in, followed by deranged shouting. At that point, there was the sending for one's mother, if you could remember who she was.

If the laces on the ball caught you in the face, there was immediately oohing and aahing from the other boys as they admired the imprint of the stitching on your face. This was disconcerting, for you knew people would stop you in the high street the following week to inquire if the surgery was successful. Worst of all, you would be referred to as Frankenstein by all those annoying seven-year-olds at school. There was no stitching on the new ball.

I was obsessed with getting this new pristine white ball like the pros used on the television. I mentioned it to my parents every time football was on. I showed them pictures of the ball and even bribed my Uncle Norman with a bottle of gin I borrowed from my dad's liquor cabinet to put in a good word for me. That part of the plan did not work so well because when he showed up at our home, he had already been hard at the bribe, and no one could tell what he was saying. I left notes next to the phone saying that our local sports store had called while my parents were out, reminding people that all the smart parents were buying their sons the new football for Christmas.

So, Christmas came: the tree lights twinkled blue and red through the tinselled branches that sparkled silver and gold in the warm firelight. The flames flickered in the grate, casting a soft yellow glow across the room. The house was both cosy and festive. I, however, was beside myself; I just had to have that new ball. I had to make sure that Christmas Day would dawn, heralding one of the greatest days of my life, and to make sure, I had to find the gifts. I knew they were hidden somewhere in the house.

My parents could be exceptionally devious when they wanted to be, like the time they told me I was going to an exercise class only to find out it was dancing lessons, and if that was not bad enough, there were girls. I was only saved by the very timely arrival of sudden onset appendicitis, which according to my overly suspicious father, was a just a bit too sudden for his liking, and questioned how it turned into sudden offset appendicitis when we were halfway home. I knew they had hidden the gifts, so I had to search high and low, which I did, but to no avail.

Eventually there was only one place left to look, the big wardrobe in my parent's bedroom. I had left this unholy place until last, hoping against hope that I wouldn't have to look there. This wardrobe was like the city of Liverpool, you did not want to go there unless you absolutely had to. It was huge, deep, and dark; the wood had been cut out of some medieval cedar tree from which highwaymen were hanged. It had knots in the panelling that looked like eyes, and in the half-light, when the wind blew, and the branches stirred outside the great window, and the moonlight filtered in upon the eerie wardrobe, it gazed at you with malevolent intent. Like the Mines of Moria, I had not wanted to go there unless there was no other way. This was no idle piece of drama. On one occasion, my parents had their bedroom redecorated. The decorator came for three days, then disappeared with the job half done. My parents told me they dismissed him for poor work, but I found an old paintbrush and a Mars bar wrapper by the wardrobe door.

There was nothing for it; I had to know, so I crept off on Christmas Eve to the only place my parents knew I would not look. I had to ensure that this would be the greatest Christmas ever. The big wardrobe door creaked open, and, with a torch in hand, I entered, knowing I would find my gift and the old decorator's skeleton. There was a heart-stopping moment when I was startled by what I thought was a legless bear, but it was only my mother's fur coat. There were shoes everywhere, it looked like Imelda Marcos had owned this wardrobe. Hey, there was my favourite comic book, the 1966 Beano Annual. I loved that book and had been frantically searching for it. My loser of a brother had spitefully put it there to get back at me for being better-looking than he was.

At long last, I came across a package that was the size and shape of a football. It was on the top shelf, and I could not reach it, but it was there all the same. I could see the tag with my name on it: 'To Jimmy from devious but loving parents.' Yes! Everything was going to be as it should be; it was going to be the best Christmas ever. I crept out of the wardrobe careful not to disturb any of my mother's rows of shoes and retreated to my room content to dream about my brand new lightweight white plastic covered authentic FA regulation football. It is all I ever wanted or would ever want.

Christmas day came, my brother sat reading his monthly magazine on the art of brass rubbing, my dad absentmindedly inquiring of my mother as to what happened to the extra bottle of gin he thought he had, and my mother, setting timers on everything so she would not detonate the Christmas dinner.

The fire was roaring and beneath the tree was my gift, my ball. We had to wait for Uncle Albert and Aunty Lillian to arrive before we could open the gifts. In due time, they arrived. The festivities had started very early for Uncle Albert, and it was already a merrier Christmas for him than it should have been. He stumbled through the door, wished everyone a merry Christmas, including the coat stand, and headed for the liquor cabinet.

Then, the moment came, minced pies were laid aside, and the hot chocolate was left to cool as we opened the presents. I had to sit through my brother, opening his gifts, a yellow sweater, and a pair of yellow pants. He was still wearing a huge, gaudy yellow ring that had come out of a Christmas cracker he had pulled with himself earlier, but I must admit that it did match his new bright yellow ensemble. Uncle Albert was delighted to be reintroduced to his old pal Johnny Walker with much seasonal glee. Then, the toe-curling, body-cringing, and nauseous experience of my mother kissing my father in appreciation for her jewelled bracelet and his new Polaroid Instamatic. That Polaroid Instamatic would later that year produce the only existing photo of a very angst-ridden and contentious event that resulted in the worst day of my father's life, as our car ended up being parked in the middle of his prized Chrysanthemums at the bottom of our garden, with a dustbin on the bonnet and the mangled wreck of my brother's bike beneath the chassis. It also provided the photo which sits in my study of my brother face down in the pebbles covered by a dozen huge angry seagulls, but all that is for later chapters. Even Aunty Lillian got in before me with a customised red and green biscuit barrel, which, according to her, was just what she wanted. I was less than convinced.

Now for what I wanted: my ball. My mother handed me my gift and attempted to kiss me, but I had become adept at sidestepping her advances, feeling I was now too old for such sentimentality. I eagerly ripped off the wrapping paper. I am not sure when it first dawned on me that something was wrong; perhaps it was when I noticed that there were countries and oceans printed on my ball and, with them, the ever-growing suspicion that it was not even a ball at all, it was a globe, a world globe. As much as it still pains me I must admit it was awesome as a globe, with countries, seas, and mountain ranges rising from its surface. As a football, it left a lot to be desired.

This was one of those defining moments in your life when you either descend into a deep depression that you never recover from or you boy up and grow a little. My mother enthusiastically told me how my geography marks would improve and how useful they would be in later life. My brother was delighted; his grin was worse than the globe, so that made my mind up for me. I decided then and there that this was a time to hide my disappointment and try at least to put a brave face on it. So, I thanked my parents and my aunt; Uncle Albert was already passed out, and I ignored my banana of a brother and sat there manfully smiling, which at least seemed to rob him of some of the pleasure he was deriving from my misery. The truth was that my boyish spirit was crushed. My dad smiled at me and ruffled my hair. I contemplated what it would be like to juggle the globe with my feet but immediately disregarded that idea. I guess this was one of the big lessons of life; we cannot always get what we want and sometimes have to learn to like what we have; if this was part of growing up, it sucked. I asked my mum when dinner would be ready; she said, "An hour."

"Where are you going?" my dad asked a little too smugly, especially after he had stood idly by and allowed my mother to ruin my life, "to have a kick around in the garden with my old tattered rubber ball from Taiwan," I replied sullenly. As I headed out, my dad said, "In that case you might need this then," throwing me a pure white plastic-coated brand-new FA regulated size five state-of-the-art football. I looked up at him and my mom; there was no need for words, my expression said it all. They both smiled and said the words every nine-year-old loves to hear..."Go play!" A piece of that ball hung on my family's Christmas tree for years as a reminder to me and my kids that disappointment is as much a part of life as success; it is how you deal with both that really matters. Kipling expressed it best when he wrote these words from his poem 'IF';

If you can dream and not make dreams your master;

If you can think and not make thoughts your aim;

If you can meet with triumph and disaster

And treat those two imposters just the same;

It was the best Christmas ever, and what was more, there were still ten more days until we had to return to school. Better still, the weather forecast predicted snow before New Year. The day after Boxing Day, it started to snow, and it snowed and snowed and snowed.

Chapter 7
Winter Break

C hristmas came and went that year with all the usual excitement and chaos. I thought I was getting a football for Christmas, but it only turned out to be a globe, which was entirely unfit for purpose, no matter how many times I kicked it against the wall. However, in the end, I did get my ball, and that Christmas became unforgettable for all the right reasons. Best of all, it started to snow on Boxing Day and didn't stop for three whole days. No other entry in the journal describes how close we all were as friends, as the entries that cover the Christmas holidays and, in particular, the snow days we spent on Old School Hill.

These were the last days of the winter holidays of 1967. The dying embers of another year glowed golden as the bright sun shone down on a white world covered by a thick blanket of snow. The day called to us to come out and play until our fingers froze and our ears were numb. 1968 waited in the frosty shadows; it would slip in and out of our lives like a familiar and much-loved friend who comes to stay until it, too, must go. Then it quietly moves on, leaving us just that little bit different than it found us. Those days passed like bright, wintry stars on a clear December night, and like kids everywhere, I was oblivious to the fact that my childhood was slipping away with them without even the merest hint of acknowledgment. The enigmatic beauty of childhood winters hid beneath their white folds all the secrets that we would carry with us into a distant future, like the magic of Christmas snow, warm fires, and mistletoe. They fired our hopes and charged our imagination and, in their passing, imprinted themselves like wondrous dreams upon our memories.

As A.E. Houseman so eloquently put it:

> Into my heart an air that kills
>
> From yon far country blows,
>
> What are those blue remembered hills
>
> What farms what spires are those.
>
> That is the land of lost content,
>
> I see it shining plain.
>
> The happy highways where I went,
>
> And cannot come again.

It would not be long before we were back at school: those long grey days of tedium, punctuated here and there by the hope of future holidays. There were still three more days until the beginning of the winter term. Three more days of unrestrained joy and pure, undefiled fun before we were forced back into those grey, self-denuding uniforms of conformity and dispatched cap in hand to the salt mines of an angst-ridden pre-adolescence. Not today, though; today, we would fill the short, sunlit hours with all the wonder that snowy days can bring to a nine-year-old.

We started on the back of the old school hill, where a morning of sledding was the order of the day. It was already teeming with boys and even a few girls, those confusing creatures that elicited in equal measure such strange and mixed feelings of magnetic attraction and stoic resistance. The snow-white hill was awash with coloured scarves, coats, and beanies as kids bundled up against the winter cold. There were boys and girls and sleds of all different shapes, speeds, and sizes careening down the quick, slick incline at various speeds and directions.

As we made our way to the top of the hill, Chippie Simpkins whizzed by on what appeared to be a greased-up plastic lid. We could not quite make out if his loud, high-pitched utterance as he flashed past us was a hail of greeting or a cry of sheer terror as he plummeted down the icy slope toward a huge pile of boys who had all ploughed into each other at the bottom of the hill. It was a vast mass of grotesquely entangled bodies. We turned just in time to see Chippie strike the mass dead centre, which resulted in both boy and plastic lid parting company. The last we saw of Chippie, was his airborne body taking flight; limbs spread like a giant black starfish disappearing into a vast white landscape.

I gazed around at the scene of unrestrained chaos. There were sleds of all kinds tin, plastic, and, of course, wood: Raif Parkinson had a very ritzy state-of-the-art cherry-infused super glider by Martel, with slick-looking stickers flaming out from both sides and a rope with which to steer. That was a distinct advantage on this hill. At the other end of the spectrum, a very rotund Jumbo Butterworth, one of the two largest boys in the school, sat at the top of the hill on a soggy piece of cardboard, trying to get himself going. Helping him were about twenty boys; their admirable if vain attempts were proving fruitless as they pushed, shoved, heaved, and pulled, all without a result. Six boys already lay prone in the snow, having succumbed to exhaustion, and poor Charlie Mossbank was slowly limping home, whimpering with what we believed to be the world's first pre-pubescent hernia. While carnage lay all around him, Jumbo just sat there finishing a ham and cheese sandwich.

The whole scene resembled a cross between a Norman Rockwell picture and Where's Waldo, except that, in this case, it was more of a Where's Chippie picture because no one had seen him for half an hour.

From the top of the hill, as one gazed out beyond the copper stream that wound its way through a copse of silver birch trees were the red brick walls of our school buildings, where come Monday morning, we would yet again assemble.

I could see our classroom by the brown mass of cardboard covering the window to the front and right of my and Wolfy's desk. The cardboard resulted from Jimmy Partington's dad's nun-chuck display when he came in for Show-and-Tell just before Christmas. The window by rights should never have been broken. The Show-and-Tell should have been stopped the first time Jimmy's dad lost control of the Asian martial arts weapon five minutes earlier when it took Miss Collingwood a full two minutes to unwrap them from around a gasping Gordon Hankin's neck. I never knew till that moment how far human eyeballs can actually come out of their sockets.

What a view it was that day from the top of old school hill. The snow, the lads, the sunshine, the sleds, the ambulances; it was all a grand sight. Then, it was time for lunch. Soon, Ginger, Wolfy, and I were sitting at my family's kitchen table, working our way through copious amounts of my mother's homemade chicken soup and bread rolls. We amused ourselves by trying to guess what the mass of dark circles and peculiar shapes were on the ceiling above our cooker. I could just make out the faintest imprint of a lamb chop in the corner and what seemed to be a dollop of corned beef hash that had been painted over at some point.

My mother was under the sink, hitting the frozen pipes with a spanner. 'Ding, Ding', she bashed away every few seconds. We did not know whether to finish our soup or come out for round three. With each assault on the pipes, there was a flurry of words that we did not understand but had my dad's name interspersed into them at regular intervals. As if summoned, he suddenly appeared in our midst with the look of a man who had just been asked to order his last meal. My mother reversed out of the sink cabinet, turned, and looked at him, her eyes narrowed, "Mend the pipes," she hissed sternly.

A look of grave resignation passed across his face, before being replaced by passive aggression. Raising himself up on his tiptoes, he raised both arms in the air in a dramatic pose that caught all our attention, spread his fingers wide, and then jabbed both hands forward, shouting, "Pipes be mended!" His sarcasm went unheeded by my mother, who ignored his gesticulation with an indifference that bordered on contempt. She turned to us, smiled gently, and asked if we wanted any more soup and rolls. "Your dad's not a very good wizard," Wolfy said quietly. We all agreed.

That afternoon, there was to be a full-on, no-holds-barred snowball fight at the local cricket field. My parents were going shopping, which did nothing to improve my father's mood. We all piled into the car so they could drop us off at the cricket field. It was just as we were pulling out that we all saw it. Gerald, the shy teen from across the road, had obviously ventured out at some point during the morning and built an impressive-looking snowman but then, like us, had gone inside for lunch. "Oh boy," my dad whispered as it came into view. My mother squealed and demanded he immediately stop the car as our attention was drawn to the snowman, as it had during the lunch break ceased to be gender neutral and had become fully male, as some young deviant had removed the large carrot nose and black coal eyes and placed them elsewhere. My mother ordered my dad to anatomically rearrange the now very healthy-looking snowman. Our laughter from the back was immediately curtailed as my mother swung around upon us like a Klingon bird of prey that had suddenly uncloaked and was about to open fire; we immediately began to stare at the floor.

After arriving at the cricket field and suiting up, a blast of snow exploding in Wolfy's ear told us that the snowball fight had already begun. This was a free-for-all. We had learned our lesson from history. The cricket ground was a much safer battleground than the last mass snowball fight, back during the freeze of '63. Back then, the skirmish involved my brother and his acquaintances. On that occasion, the venue was the old railway line. Railway tracks, unlike cricket fields, which have grass under the snow, had gravel instead, which annoyingly infiltrated the snowballs. After that fight, nothing was the same again. My brother had volunteered to referee the snowball fight for some insane reason. So, like a baby wildebeest born with red and white concentric circles on its chest, he stood in the centre of a ring of seventy-five well-armed boys and declared the battle begun. He later told one of his therapists that he was genuinely surprised when the first seventy-five gravel-filled snowballs hit him simultaneously, which resulted in a severe physical pummelling and great emotional trauma, which, as my dad continually bemoaned, made countless therapists very rich men.

The first wave of fighting was fierce and vindictive, as every wrong for the past year was put right, and every petty grievance was avenged. These ran from cutting in at the milk line at school to sending forged love notes, supposedly signed by you, to the most frightening girl in school. This, in turn, resulted in a year of hiding in closets and cupboards, which in turn created a fear of dark places and nervous paralysis when the random draw for the school dance cards was made. Punishment for the poring of lumpy custard into one's satchel had to be meted out, and the snitching to your mother when you attempted the unofficial school record of eating 17 prunes in one sitting, followed by 17 seconds of breaking another school record, getting them out again.

Weary after venting our spleen upon all these misguided miscreants, the numbers thinned out until we were in sole ownership of the cricket field. We claimed a rightful Victory! The following rest period found us sitting on the fence at the end of the field named after one of our village's fast bowlers, Reginald J Bell, the last of the moustachioed musketeers of 1911, many of whom were gone now, having given their lives for their country on other battlefields, in Flanders and the Somme, where the ammunition was infinitely more deadly than snowballs.

So, it was that evening in late December 1967 that we sat on the fence at the ill-named Bell End, watching the sky catch fire at the close of day. The dipping sun bathed the field in a deep crimson hue, which reflected off the snow in a soft and redolent glow. There in the gathering gloom of that winter dusk, as the dark earth gave way to darker shadows, we talked and laughed at the silliest of things, each one of us lost in another life now far re-moved from this one. I remember the streetlights coming on, flickering momentarily, and then blazing into light. That was the universal sign that it was time to go home. If you were out after the lights came on mothers began to fret, imagining all sorts of horrible things. The same thoughts also crossed your brother's mind but elicited an entire-ly different response to the manic worry manifest in our mothers. Phone calls and search parties would occur until the recalcitrant or absent-minded child was found. It is then that you were soundly thrashed by a weeping woman, who, all the time she is inflicting bodily pain on you, is telling you how the beating is hurting her much more than you, which I very much doubted. She also reproaches you for being a thoughtless, mindless, selfish little insect while at the same time asking you if you want your favourite tea when the thrashing is over.

Your brother, however, is manfully hiding his disappoint-ment that you have been found, and even greater disap-pointment that they brought you back, instead of dropping you off at a home for wayward boys. He acts familiarly but it is with meretricious and fleeting concern.

In the years to come, when I had occasion to go home to visit family, I would often walk down to the cricket field. Nothing has changed much in the last fifty years. I always walk down to the fence we sat on that night and gaze out over the fields and woods. I do not have to remember that day; all I have to do is listen, and I can hear us all once more as we were then, on that night, all those years ago. I can hear them all, all those distantly familiar voices that belong now to another time, like echoes from a cherished past drifting down the years, carrying a message from a world that is now long gone to one that is yet to be. They whisper to us all, 'Time and tide wait for no man.'

That night, too, we came home tired and cold and grateful to see the warm yellow glow emitting from the front windows of our houses. It told me that all was well and as it should be. At my house, I stopped momentarily at the door and shrugged absentmindedly against the cool chill of the still winter evening. Looking up into that clear cold sky as the first stars appeared, I smiled—it had been a grand day.

January came all too soon, and with it 1968 arrived in our lives. We were back in school before we knew it. If that was not traumatic enough for a young lad, then what happened next would not only scare the living Evian out of me but also threaten our house's continued fuel supply.

January 1968

Chapter 8
Shed of the Undead

⸻◆◇◆⸻

It was January 1968, the new year had slipped quietly in while no one was looking, and it would bide with us a while until it too would make its exit, leaving us with its own unique legacy that would in some small way help shape and define who we were yet to be. The snow had melted, taking with it the all too brief winter wonderland that had transported us, if for a little, while out of the ordinary, before returning us again to the slate grey typicality of everyday life.

Sunday afternoons in 1968 were a deadly dull affair for a boy of nine. It is especially galling when your mother watches ice skating on the house's only black and white television set, especially as football was on the other channel. My mother yelped intermittently every time either the skaters jumped, or I moved and screwed up the picture. I had been made to stand in the corner next to the television and hold up the indoor aerial so my mother could have the perfect picture.

I was tired of my arm aching from holding this glorified coat hanger in the air like some juvenile Statue of Liberty. I was also tired of being shouted at whenever the picture went weird. It was very irritating because my brother was yelling at me not to move yet throwing large pieces of Lego at my head when no one was looking. I had complained about this to my mother so often during the skating that, at one point, she broke off from her skating fascination to fix an icy glare upon me that carried with it more than a hint of menace. That was it. I knew the next word out of my mouth would bring her off that couch like the multi-headed hydra of antiquity, bent on destroying anything annoying it, so I kept quiet.

I was considering quoting the child labour laws about cruel and unusual punishment of minors when my hand slipped, and the screen went all snowy, just as Irena Rodnina had been flung into the air by Alexander Zeitsev. There was a corporate groan around the room and an anguished cry from my mother, "James David," the use of both my Christian names was never a good thing. Then came those warm and encouraging words of brotherly love: "Look what you have done now, frog face!" yelled my brother, "you have ruined it for all of us," he cried as he hurled a huge plastic construction brick at my head.

By the time I had contorted myself back into the correct position, they were scraping Miss Rodnina off the ice, and my mother's afternoon had been ruined. I was told in no uncertain terms that I had no future as an aerial holder if that was the career I chose to pursue in later years. My mother, fighting hard to preserve all the protective instincts of motherhood in order not to eat her youngest, ordered me to sit quietly in a chair for ten minutes and rethink my life. My father stuck his head around the door and asked how everything was going, but then very quickly gauged my mother's mood and retreated back to the garden shed.

Later that evening, my brother, who was now sitting at the dining room table attempting to do his homework, had graduated from throwing Legos at me to throwing sugared almonds from the bowl on the table.

Enough was enough. I wasn't going to be continually pillo-ried by someone who was having difficulty trying to work out how his ballpoint pen worked. I gathered a handful of the nuts from the ones he had tossed at me and decided that unleashing all of them at once at his big fat head was the best strategy, well, almost the best strategy. Unluckily for me, my father walked in just as they nailed him. Noticing my father's presence, he immediately threw himself off his chair, wailing like a banshee. He writhed around on the floor, yelling like he was about to give birth, while my dad gazed at me intently. "Front room, now!" he said in the same calm, ominous tone that judges used when donning the black cap and sentencing some devious character to the gallows. I got up and immediately proceeded to the front room, gazing down at the face of evil as it grinned up at me from the carpet and winked.

The front room of our house was awesome. It had a huge bay window and a massive fireplace with a deep mantle upon which sat an ornately crafted carriage clock that was either like my brother, very slow, or for some reason set to Hong Kong time. In the room, there were two large, deep, pillowy leather chairs and a long couch. Above the fireplace hung my father's pride and joy, a Vermeer painting of a startled woman who seemed to have lost an earring. It was a room my parents used for entertaining guests and insur-ance salesmen. It also contained the liquor cabinet, which still had scratch marks on the door from Uncle Albert's fingernails after my dad had locked it for everyone's safety the previous Christmas. It was also the room to which we were summoned when the game was up, and we had been caught or found out, like now. My father sat in his favourite leather wingback chair and held court. He was both judge and jury and often times executioner as well.

He demanded an account of what had transpired, so I told him everything. He acknowledged the mitigating circumstances of being forced to stand with my arm in the air for a long period of time while being made to watch figure skating. There was, for a moment, a genuine look of empathy and compassion in his eyes, but then it was gone in an instant when the sugared almonds were mentioned. The verdict was guilty, but under extreme provocation, my sentence was commuted to a stern reprimand and the vacuuming of the living room floor.

I knew something was wrong some weeks later when my parents were unusually nice to me, and my brother looked like a feline who had recently devoured a small bird. Then they dropped the bombshell as my mother loaded my plate with more chips. Apparently, they had to attend a work dinner at my dad's company, meaning I was to be babysat by my brother. "Is he okay?" I heard my dad's voice as if far away through the misty veil encompassing me. "He's fine," my mother said with the tone of a woman who didn't quite believe what she was saying.

I only had one chore in those days, but it was significant. My job was to keep the coal scuttle filled so my parents didn't have to go outside to gather winter fuel. Central heating had not yet arrived at our house, so we had open fires in all the rooms except the bedrooms unless required. Coal had been outlawed a couple of years before because it killed more people than the bubonic plague and school dinners combined. So now there was coke, a kind of coal, but with the impurities removed. The coke was stored in the old coal shed at the bottom of the garden, beyond the outhouse, the laundry room, and the tool shed, many yards away from humanity.

It was a cold, dark, and forbidding place with no light because my dad never changed the bulb despite continued promises to the contrary. At night, I had to go down there and enter that piteous enclave of black silent eeriness, shovel a couple of scoops into the scuttle, and haul it back to the house. It was bad enough during the day, but at night, it was the worst, for all types of unholy things were holed up in that coal shed.

I should have known something was wrong by how nice my brother was to me. My parents left for their dinner with their customary threats to both of us, and then they were gone. I usually had to go to bed at eight o'clock, but my brother let me stay up longer; this was something he never did. The clock rang nine, and still, he didn't make me go to bed; something was afoot. At 9:25 pm he asked me if I wanted to watch a show called '*Hammer House*'. He didn't finish the full title of the program due to the utter infamy of his sneaky rodent-like character. I said, "Yes." He knew I would do anything to stay up longer, so we watched '*Dracula, Prince of the Night*,' starring Christopher Lee as the fanged one. I watched the whole thing.

By the time it had ended, I had chewed my way through my mother's favourite pillow, which I was hiding behind. I asked my brother if it was true, and he nodded affirmatively. He then added that it was a well-known fact that for three weeks every January, Dracula chose a coal shed in our area to inhabit until he moved further north in search of fresh blood. He said he looked for houses with dark coal sheds at the end of the garden. That sounded very plausible to me.

"What is wrong with him?" my dad said the next evening when he asked me to go fetch the coke for the fire. "No!" I replied sternly, "And you can't make me."

"Is it those damn cats?" My father inquired of my mother, like she had the answer to everything. He was referring to a bunch of rather despicable and degenerate feral cats that had taken residence under old man Fanshaw's garden shed next door. They were particularly cunning and vicious, given to hunting in packs. A small boy needed all his wits about him when retrieving his football, which had accidentally strayed over the fence into Fanshaw's garden. It had become so bad that I had to ask Wolfy to spot for me from the bedroom window. They moved and struck like velociraptors; you didn't see them until you became lunch. The cats struck with awesome speed and ferocity. It required special equipment to retrieve one's ball. A motorbike helmet, thick leather gloves, cricket pads and a nine iron just to get your ball back and stay in one piece.

The story goes that old man Fanshaw had called in an unsuspecting county animal control worker to come and deal with this crazed brood of demented felines. Safe to say, he seriously underestimated the situation and was far too complacent. Years later, after he had begun to recover from the ordeal and was taking solid food again, the county worker recounted the story of that fateful afternoon when seeing four sweet kitties on the lawn he had relaxed just for a moment, failing to see the five lurking menacingly on the garage roof, ears back tails wagging, spitting, and hissing. It was a scene reminiscent of our local village council meetings. It was all over in a matter of seconds. "I was lucky to survive," he is said to have shouted wildly over and over as he tried to tell the story, only to slide into a deep catatonic state.

After spending many years in a home for demented government workers just outside of Southport, where the inmates were forced to listen to Barry Manilow songs and fed bowls of Valium-laced oxtail soup, he improved and was allowed out again. By all accounts, he was doing very well until he accidentally strolled into that petting zoo.

My father demanded to know why I would rather do my homework or, clean out the pantry, or even risk the front room rather than go to the coal shed. This small, insignificant issue became a major incident. It was only when he threatened not to take me to Station Road to watch the rugby that I decided to fess up to what was going on. Even the iron will of a petrified nine-year-old has its breaking point and not going to watch Swinton play with my dad and Uncle Wilf was one of them. My father patiently asked me again why I wouldn't go to the coal shed. "Because Christopher Lee is living in there," I said defiantly. It's one of the only times I have seen my father completely speechless. The swiftly changing expressions on his face denoted the thought that by some freak dimensional shift, he had found himself momentarily transported into a surreal world deep in an alternate universe.

My mother smiled at me and said softly," Why don't you tell us the whole story? "So, I did! My brother attempted to creep out of the room, but my dad, sensing him to be complicit in all this and having, as he always said, 'eyes in the back of his head', arrested him with the word "Freeze!" I told the story of being allowed to stay up and watch the 'Hammer House of Horrors.' It was at this moment that I realised my brother had a possible career as an actor if he lived that long. He was looking directly at me over my dad's shoulder, and his face was contorting through a series of expressions that ran the full gamut of emotions. He was attempting communication without uttering a single word. First, there was the look of menace, then threat, as I continued my story before the entreating began, from there he moved to pleading (I liked that one) and begging, then to resignation, which now having come full circle spawned both hostility and hatred as I finished my account. My father turned slowly and ominously toward him; with eyebrows furrowed, he fixed him with that all too familiar icy glare. "Front room," we all said in unison.

It was at this moment that I came to understand how cool dads are, and that men have a different way of speaking. Mothers' love us but don't always relate to us on the same level as a man; this was a prime example. My mother began by telling me that Christopher Lee was not living in our coal shed, that there was no such thing as vampires or portable coffins, and if there were, they wouldn't fit in the coal shed. She finished her summary by telling me that I really shouldn't be so silly and that I should get over it and go and wash my neck. I was less than convinced. I loved my mother, but what did she know about these things? Plus, she wouldn't be able to drive a stake through Christopher Lee's heart so we could get coke and keep the house heated.

My dad figured I was less than convinced, so he sat beside me. Even to this day, I admire how he could, as ancient as he was, engage in nine-year-old speak. "Dracula isn't in our shed," he said to me.

"Why?" I asked.

"Number of reasons," he said softly. "Firstly, the feral cats next door would not stand for a bat living in our shed and would shred it, supernatural or not," he said. "Second, vampires don't like broccoli; they can't stand it," he said. This made sense; I had never wanted to be in the same room with it. "I will place broccoli all over the shed," he said knowingly, shaking his head, "He won't come near".

"And thirdly?" I asked. He smiled,

"Vampires rarely ever leave Yorkshire," he said, nodding his head affirmatively. "So..." he slapped me on the back and winked at me, "You are completely safe."

I thought this would be the end of it, but it wasn't. I asked my dad what punishment my brother would receive, and he told me to mind my own business or I would get the same. I suggested sending him to Devil's Island might be a good idea. My father glared at me, and I backed off. "The French just closed it," he muttered as he went off into the front room. My brother, being of low character, did not forget nor did he forgive, and waited for his revenge. After he had served his time, which only seemed to feed his vitriol, he was back, and there was a disturbed look about him.

One day, as it came close to the time to bring in the coke from the coal shed, I saw him lurking down by the end of the garden. He kept looking furtively up the path every few minutes and suddenly disappeared. It didn't take the brain of Britain to work out that he was up to no good. I couldn't see him anywhere but guessed he had hidden himself in the coal shed, ready to pounce on me when I went in and scare the Evian out of me. That evening, I told my dad I had hurt my wrist getting the top of a Shandy bottle and asked if he could get the coke tonight. He said, "Yes". He was in a good mood. I remember him whistling as he walked out of the house, the scuttle swinging in his hand as he went his merry way.

The twilight had given way to the encroaching night, and by now it was pitch black out there. However, my dad, in good spirits, made his way to the coal shed. He turned the corner and went into the shed. A second later, there was a shriek followed by a louder, deeper, stronger yell and the sound of the scuttle hitting the ceiling. There was a scampering of feet, and my wide-eyed brother appeared looking panicked and more ashen than his usual pasty self, highlighting the black smudges all over his face. My dad then appeared; he looked older somehow, and the new grey hair he had just acquired suited him. He, too, was pale and breathing hard, as I watched him swig down half a bottle of my mother's cooking sherry. He was fighting hard to compose himself. My mother came in and said what she always said, "What on earth?" She never finished that sentence. When my dad stopped shaking and the wild look of terror had subsided, there was only one thing to be said to my brother, "Front room!".

I suffered from PCLSD for many years after that. My 'Post Christopher Lee Stress Disorder' could come upon me at any time. It took three bags of frozen broccoli and my wife's favourite pillow before I could watch Fellowship of the Rings with my kids, and even then the sudden 20-foot big screen close up of him triggered my PCLSD, and my right hand froze in the popcorn bucket, try as they might my kids couldn't remove it and so they went popcorn-less for the entire movie. They never watched it with me again.

Having escaped the clutches of Christopher Lee, well, at least for the time being, it seemed the jeopardy was over, and I could breathe easier. However, as January turned into February, my life was to take a turn for the worse as what I thought to be an ingenious ploy to win Cynthia Hardcastle's affections would ultimately land me in serious trouble, all because of a tube of smarties and a horse.

February

Chapter 9
The Trial

———◆○◆———

Having recovered from my brother's attempt to frighten me to death, everything settled back down to as mundane as life could possibly be for a nine-year-old. It wouldn't last long. As the cold winds of January blew us into an even colder February that year, things were starting to look up for me until it all went drastically wrong.

It all started with shopping. It was Saturday when my parents did the weekly shopping, which was always an adventure, especially where my mother was concerned. After two hours of shopping, she invariably arrived at the checkout only to discover that somewhere along the way, she had acquired another shopping trolly, somebody else's trolly. This time, it had two sixty-pound bags of birdseed, three packets of suppositories, two cases of cottage cheese, and four packets of Rye Vita.

My dad would then be dispatched throughout the store to find the abandoned trolley with all our groceries in it, while at the same time trying to avoid anyone who might have previously owned the trolley my mother now possessed. Judging by the cart's contents, he would have to avoid anyone very thin, walking rather gingerly and having a large parrot on one shoulder.

After this mayhem, my dad liked to take my mother for lunch at the local Civic Hall next door, which was a rather posh restaurant with tablecloths, nice music, and real silverware. A mezzanine surrounded the restaurant about twenty feet above the tables immediately below. As I had been eating steadily all morning and still working my way through a tube of Smarties, I was despatched to the mezzanine to wait till my parents were finished with their meal.

I wanted to see what everyone seated at the tables immediately below was eating, so I leaned over the railing on the mezzanine, except that I leaned a little too far over the rail, which caused my smarties to fall out of the tube. Numerous smarties falling from twenty feet can make quite a splash when they hit a bowl of tomato soup, as the lady directly beneath me discovered when it happened to her. The splashes created a huge red stain on her pristine white blouse. She screamed and jumped up from the table as waiters rushed to her aid. The soup was in her face and hair, as well as all over the front of her clothing; she looked like the only survivor from the St Valentines Day massacre as she stumbled around hysterically. It was a while before anyone could figure out what had happened, by which time all the incriminating evidence had been disposed of in the nearby bin, and I was halfway down the staircase. My parents, instinctively suspecting that I was somehow complicit in all this, alighted their table quietly, paid, and also headed for the exit without having their dessert.

Miffed at missing out on his jam roll and custard, my dad told my mother that I needed to go with her the following day when she visited my aunt. This was a dire and severe punishment for what was clearly an accident.

That was how it all started, for had I not been there as planned that Sunday, I would never have been caught writing a love note to Cynthia Hardcastle, who was quite clearly a girl. As such, I had violated the first four rules of our gang law by fraternising with her.

The penalty for fraternising with girls was severe, to say the least, especially if you were to be found guilty by the tribunal. In those far-off days, a tribunal comprised a court-appointed prosecutor and three judges. These were solemn proceedings, and every gang member was present. You had to defend yourself, and if your defence failed and you were found guilty, the presiding judge would put on a black cap and pronounce a sentence of banishment. We didn't have a black cap, so we used a black and white beanie that Limpy's mother had knitted and had Bolton Wonderers misspelled on the front. It lay on a shelf in the den, a constant and sobering reminder to all who gazed upon it of the swift and merciless end that could come to any of us who transgressed the rules. I had been charged with breaking the Prime Directive, which incorporated the first four rules, and was, therefore, in danger of four banishments to be served consecutively, which meant I would be ninety-two by the time I was allowed back into the den.

It all started, as most of my troubles did when I devised a plan of such cunning genius that it could not fail. I could and should have blamed it on my Uncle Albert because it was most definitely all his fault. My mother had, as my dad requested, carted me off the next day, a dismal, rainy Sunday afternoon, to Uncle Albert and Aunty Lillian's house. These were the days that tried the souls of men and small boys, especially small boys. It was four hours of torture akin to the Spanish Inquisition. My brother and my dad were somehow exempt from this dreaded experience. My dad always said something I did not understand about pliers and fingernails, and my brother said he had homework;

I, too, would have been excused except for those infernal smarties.

So, off we went to Uncle Albert and Aunty Lillian's house dressed in my Sunday best, with enough Brylcreem on my hair to grease an indoor toboggan run. Dragged into the parlour, my mother made me sit on an old ottoman by the fire as I was forced to listen to a litany of mind-numbing tittle-tattle about people I barely knew. The first subject of conversation was Great Uncle Roy, who was a topic of great interest to the two women. A man who, according to Aunty Lillian, got lost in his own garden. There were hushed tones when they discussed how something strange happened to Cousin Phyllis, but I never knew what it was as my mother never finished her sentences, mouthing to my aunt in silent words, each one emphasized with an absurdly dramatic facial expression. I thought it was a game at first but realised that the strategic silences were because of young and delicate ears. I picked up enough to work out that Phyllis's boyfriend had made her put on a lot of weight over the last few months, and, that she was expecting something, and that it was to be delivered by November. I knew the Royal Mail was slow, but November, sheesh!

I also learned all about Mrs. Haskell's varicose veins. Apparently, her left leg could now pass as a road map of Greater Manchester. I also learned about goitres, gallstones, lumbago, sciatica, and water on the knee. There was a supposedly very juicy story about Mr. Brown from number forty-two that Aunty Lillian just had to share, and apparently, this must have been remarkably interesting as my mother uttered, "Oh yes," and leaned in so as not to miss any of the details. Again, there were large gaps in the conversation as the women mouthed the silent words, rolled their eyes, and shook their heads.

Apparently, Mr. Brown had to climb out of his best friend's bedroom window when his friend had come home early from work one day. It seems he had slipped on the wet tile while attempting to put his pants on and had gone hurtling down the roof and into the drainpipe, catapulting himself over the gutter and landing in the bushes twenty feet below. Aunty Lillian had it on good authority that it took the ambulance men half an hour to extricate him from the shrubs and that he had severely injured something. I do not know what he had injured because it all went silent at that point, and there was a lot of wincing. My mother's expression intimated something very unpleasant indeed.

This is how it went, hour upon eternal hour. Uncle Albert was asleep in the chair. Obviously, at some point in the proceedings, he had been fortunate enough to have lapsed into unconsciousness. The rain beat down in a steady rhythm on the windowpane; the grandfather clock beat a constant tick-tock; the fire crackled in the grate; all the while, I sat upon the old ottoman as the women talked and talked and talked. I wondered if anyone had ever died of boredom, but immediately dismissed that as improbable as twenty thousand people watched Bolton Wanderers play every week and went safely home afterward. I stared into the red glowing embers of the fire until my mother scolded me by stating that I would go blind and have to spend my life sitting on a street corner in the snow selling paper roses. She asked if I wanted that, and I said, "No," while wondering where she got these things from.

I then had a staring contest with Archie, Uncle Albert's dog, which I kept losing. I later discovered that Archie slept with his eyes open, which was very cool. Sleeping with your eyes open would have certainly made even school bearable. I often thought that my dad had mastered this art when my mother recounted one of her nights playing Bingo.

At last, Uncle Albert woke up shouting, "I know nothing about it," before he realised where he was. He then picked up the paper. It was at that precise moment that my life nearly changed forever, for it was in response to his question that my whole future hung in the balance.

He rifled through the paper until he found the racing pages, then asked me what I fancied in the two-thirty at Kempton Park the next day. I knew nothing about horse racing except that it was boring, so I asked him the names. He read them all out, with their odds. I said I fancied 'Slackers Surge' at eighteen to one against. He eyed me with a dubious yet quizzical look; I just smiled. "By Jove, I will have a tenner on it," he cried with gusto, and as the firelight glinted off his spectacles, he declared, "I think the boy has the rights of it!"

Well, as it turned out, the boy did have the rights of it, and the horse won by two lengths. It won Uncle Albert the princely sum of one hundred and eighty pounds, translated into today's currency, close to three thousand pounds. That horse was the cause of all my problems. When I came home the following Thursday, my mother informed me that Uncle Albert and Auntie Lillian had visited. They had invited my mom and dad on an all-expenses-paid weekend trip to London out of the booty he had gained from my pick. She told me he had left a large gift for me in the front room.

I tore the paper off, and there it was, a brand new 'The Man from U.N.C.L.E.' spy kit with extra stuff. This was the best ever. Which kid in those days did not like 'The Man from U.N.C.L.E.' and watched it at every opportunity? I really liked Napoleon Solo; he was my hero at the time. The large box had everything: guns, badges, communicators, the U.N.C.L.E. pin, and a pair of handcuffs. Best of all was 'The Man from U.N.C.L.E.' invisible ink pen. No one else had one of these sets. I would be the talk of milk time. On the box was a note from Uncle Albert saying, "Thanks, kid, what do you fancy for the four-fifteen at Doncaster on Saturday?" I was moved by his touching note. This was awesome. I would be St. Matthews' answer to Napoleon Solo. The detailed description of all the gizmos in the kit revealed in the journal indicates just how special it was to have one of these at that age.

The invisible ink pen gave me an idea that I considered fool-proof. I would write a love letter to Cynthia Hardcastle out-lining my intentions. My ingenuity and Robert Vaughn-like appeal would so sweep her away that she would become my secret girlfriend. It was a flawless plan. I took the paper and waxed eloquent, declaring in ink that no one would see: "You are almost better than football and Meccano. I will fix your bike and capture tadpoles for you. I love you, Cynthia Hardcastle," then I signed it. Such rosy prose would be impossible to resist, rendering her heart incapable of loving anyone but me. The best part was that no one would ever know; there would be no evidence. I scribbled it off lightly and checked it; sure enough, the paper was blank. Only she and I would ever know about the hidden message. I folded it up and headed into the playground to deliver my declaration of love, invisibly, of course.

I approached Cynthia and her two scary sidekicks: Henri-etta Pross, a gangly squib of a girl with a mean disposition and vitriolic nature, who, I believe, in later life became very successful and rose quickly through the ranks of the Inland Revenue Service. The other one was called Ophelia Pitt Brown. She was a very snooty girl and had a way of making you feel like you trod in something on the way over to talk to them. She was the type of girl who frightened young boys and small pets. She eventually married some poor tyke called Reginald, who sadly must have inadvertently upset a caravan full of travellers early in his young life. Apparently, one night in 1987, she threw a dinner party after he and Ophelia had been married a few years. The entertainment that night included a game of hide and seek. He went and hid with the rest of them, but, according to rumour, they did not find him until 2005, hiding in a bar in Caracas. The locals there referred to him as "Tres unfortuno Crocadillo," or loosely translated, "one who has peered deep and long into the throat of the crocodile."

There she was, looking all goddess-like, Cynthia Hardcastle, standing like Aphrodite between two gorgons. "I think you dropped this," I declared to all in a strong and stentorian voice. I handed her the note and then walked away. I was basking in the glow of self-approbation when I realised with horror that my plan was not quite as perfect as I thought. It had become clear to me in a moment of rare and brief lucidity that even though it was true, no one could read the note, that also included Cynthia herself. I ran back to get the note when, to my deep consternation, I saw her give my note to Beaky, telling him to give it back to me and that she did not appreciate practical jokes.

The next thing I knew, I was on trial for breaking the first four rules of our fraternity. To make matters worse, Billingsley was presiding. The den was full. News had gotten out about my flagrant violation of gang law. It was a capacity crowd, with me front and centre. There before me was the half-burned document on the table.

Beaky had smelled a rat when Cynthia gave him the note. He also smelled the paper and saw the light imprint. To the

utter infamy of his nosey name, he had investigated the
matter further. He, Murphy, Ginger, and Wolfy had heated
the paper from underneath with an open flame, illuminat-
ing the writing and laying it all out for everyone to see.
Luckily for me, Wolfy had gotten overly excited at one point
in the findings and held the match too closely, setting fire
to the note. Mercifully, he had managed to burn the part of
the note with Cynthia's name on it. The circumstantial evidence, however, was overwhelming. Beaky was appearing
for the prosecution, which was indeed frightening, as he
was by far the brightest of us all, which, while not saying
much, was going to pose a problem. This was not going to
be easy.

The trial began with great trepidation, especially on my
part. Beaky opened for the prosecution. "Have you been
sending notes to that girl?" he said, with too much mal-
ice for my liking. He used the term 'that girl', for uttering
the name of a girl in the den violated the sanctity of our
hallowed headquarters. Just as "Macbeth" must not be
uttered in a theatre for fear of bringing bad luck, so a girl's
name must never be invoked inside the den. The last time
a girl's name had been spoken in the den, our meeting
place had been partially destroyed less than twenty-four
hours later when twenty-two local cricketers from the adjacent cricket field climbed the fence and came looking for
their ball after big Kenny Worthington, the village plumber,
had hit a particularly impressive six over backward square
leg. The den, having been built by digging into the side
of the railway embankment by a bunch of nine-year-old
boys, was a little light on architectural design and structural
integrity. Consequently, its safety features were non-exis-
tent. That serial herd of clodhopping cricketers had stam-
peded across our roof, causing it to collapse. We did, in
time, rebuild it and, in doing so, found the lost cricket ball,

which, from that moment on, sat in the centre of our den as a perpetual reminder to us all when in the den, not to mention any girl's names or move too suddenly.

Meanwhile, Beaky was warming to his task, "Is this your note?" he yelled at me, holding up the severely singed note for all to see. "Yes," I replied confidently.

"To whom was the note written?" He drew the word whom out dramatically.

"To my mother," I stated defiantly. I had decided that my only defence was to lie through my teeth.

"Your mother?" he repeated incredulously.

"Yes, my mother," I replied again. I had decided that every-one there, except possibly Wolfy, was of woman-born, and therefore, the mother defence was my best option.

"Why would you write a love note to your mother?" he replied.

"Because I love her," I spluttered.

"Why would you write a love note to your mother telling her you loved her in invisible ink?" he continued. "She wouldn't be able to read it."

"I know," I said. He had me there. My dad said no one could defend an absurdly indefensible position better than me, so that was my plan.

"Why would you write a blank love note to your moth-er if she couldn't read it?" he persisted. He was right, of course; my mother's knowledge of 'The Man from U.N.C.L. E.' paraphernalia was pitiful and sadly lacking. I had to think quickly; she would never have added heat to the note and deciphered the message. "That's the point," I said loudly.

"What is?" he retorted. I continued,

"No boy our age tells his mother he loves her out loud." There was a murmur of approval from the gallery. It was a universal truth that the average lad would rather eat broccoli while watching *Panorama* than be caught speaking sweet affections to his mother in public.

I was getting up a head of steam. "Let me get this right," Beaky said. "You wrote a love note to your mother in invisible ink so she wouldn't be able to read it?"

"Yes," I replied. Beaky smiled,

"Then why did you give it to that girl then?" he continued.

"To give to my mother" I replied.

"Does she know your mother?" Beaky hammered back, scenting blood in the water,

"No," I gulped back feebly. There was a definite sense that the vultures were beginning to circle. There was quiet mumbling, and most of the lads looked gravely at the floor; this wasn't going well. Beaky took a deep breath and raised himself to deliver the coup de gras. He stooped low and, pivoting on one foot, took in the entire gaze of the audience, declaring to all in a slow, high-pitched voice, "Are you telling us that you gave a love note meant for your mother, which she cannot read, to a girl she did not know, so that she could receive sentiments that you didn't want her to see?" he cried theatrically while posturing for the sake of effect.

"Precisely," I replied, with all the confidence of a steerage class passenger on the Titanic inquiring as to what that bump was. Then, in the bemused silence that followed, I sat down.

The judges convened outside, on the top of the embankment, casually discussing my fate while they threw rocks at an empty Tizer can on the railway line below. My whole life hung in the balance. If the verdict went against me, the consequences were unthinkable. I would be consigned to play with the sops, fops, and swots at playtime, never more to sit with the lads behind the bike shed discussing the pros and cons of the sweeper system and the continued biological evolution of Teddy Fothergill's sister. Furthermore, there would have been no more football on Saturday mornings; I would have to go shopping with my mother and my martyr of a father, who aged visibly with every four-hour trip to the store. Desperate times called for desperate measures.

In my closing remarks, I had inadvertently, and accidentally on purpose, mentioned that the gang enjoyed hanging out at my house, using my rope swing, our T.V. nights, my mother's cookies, having access to my Subbuteo table, and our backyard with the full-size goals, and play area. These somehow accidentally slipped into my summation. Despite Beaky yelling objection, the judges listened. Based on my closing arguments, it took the judges only two minutes to decide on a verdict of 'not guilty by reason of insufficient evidence, as there was no name on the letter the case was inconclusive.' There was much rejoicing, and we pooled our money, which came to a whopping three shillings and sixpence, which helped us buy ten Sherbet fountains, with which we celebrated my great escape.

The trial was over. I had been acquitted and could now rejoin my pals. All was right with the world once more. That day, I vowed never again to write a note in invisible ink and solemnly held to that vow for all these years. Cynthia Hardcastle did not speak to me for the rest of that term.

Forty-seven years later, I attended a fundraising dinner in Los Angeles. The auction commenced, and the audience grew incredibly quiet as the bidding began. Suddenly, a cell phone went off, breaking the silence. The ringtone was the theme from the movie The Magnificent Seven; everyone turned to see whose phone it was that had so rudely interrupted the proceedings. There sat a sheepish-looking Robert Vaughn, with cell phone half raised, smiling apologetically. The room instantly broke into a mixture of laughter and applause. Later that evening, I briefly chatted with Napoleon Solo himself. We said goodnight, and The Man from U.N.C.L.E. shook my hand. Who would have thought?!

The rest of February passed peacefully and without incident. Winter was releasing its icy grip as the long-awaited spring began to emerge in flashes of yellow daffodils and tulips, which blazed blue, white, and sunset red against the green waking earth. They brought a sense of hope and expectation as the slowly strengthening sun hinted at warmer days. That third week of March filled us with excitement and anticipation, as it was the time of year when the Wakes came to town.

March

Chapter 10
The Wakes

The Funfair had come to town. It was truly a carnival atmosphere that came once a year every spring when the gusting March winds were blowing themselves out. The month that had come in like a lion was now leaving like a lamb, as the soft spring zephyrs replaced the roaring gusts and marked the turning of the year and, with it, the promise of new life.

The Wakes were always loud and busy. Throngs of people bustled through the narrow passages as the dazzling lights flashed and spun amidst the whirring mechanical rides and quickly erected stalls and tents. Here, you could ride the rides, play hoopla, pop darts, or shoot air rifles to your heart's content. You could win coconuts, goldfish, and all kinds of plastic animals and strange prizes. It was an intriguing and exciting experience for us kids and it only came once a year. The sights, sounds, and smells of the Wakes filled us with a sense of wonder. The rides really were an adrenaline rush, mainly because of the way they were constructed; any ride could quite easily be your last. Exciting things were always happening at the fair, like ride owners running across the backfields being chased by men with warrants. These were grand nights of adventure not to be missed, even if it did mean all of us travelling on a Lancashire County transport bus.

These fairs, or wakes, as we called them, had been around for a long time. The first recorded fair in England was in 1133. It was a lot less fun, of course. People got to throw a potato at the vicar and then take off to the refreshment hut, where they stuck a red-hot poker in their mead, took a swig, and went home. As the centuries passed, it became more fun as the first mechanised rides were introduced. These were the forerunners of the modern-day Waltzers. Back then, you and your good woman would sit on the seats of the wooden contraption and be propelled around just as fast as the kids from the poor house could pedal. The flashing lights consisted of a peasant running alongside your seat, covering and uncovering a lit candle as fast as possible. If you got lucky and started to make out with your wench, then the vicar would appear and commence to throw potatoes at you.

By the eighteen hundreds, the industrial age had dawned; workers in cities all over the country fed up with working sixteen-hour days for fifty-two weeks a year began to take an unofficial week off each May. Only in Liverpool did they work that week so they could continue to take the other fifty-one weeks off. This week became known as Wakes Week when thousands of people from the cities descended on seaside resorts like Blackpool to drink, dance, and throw potatoes at each other. Not everyone could get to Blackpool and other coastal resorts, so all the glitz and glamour of Blackpool came to all the people in the little towns and villages around the country. So it was that the funfairs evolved into the iconic local week of amusements and frivolity that marked people's lives for centuries, right on into the late 1960s.

It was then, with an air of excitement and anticipation, that our entire gang gathered at the bus stop at the end of our road. In those days, the world was different; children flew out the door in the morning to play on the village green, in the local woods, or on the nearby railway line without a second thought as to any possible danger except natural hazards. These natural hazards included such things as falling out of trees, being hit by a ten-ton locomotive, getting mauled in a frenzied ruck playing rugby, being buried alive in a half-built den, sailing a home-built raft across the local lake, or being hunted by a clowder of demented cats.

However, despite the intrinsic danger of a boy's world, it was, to all intent and purpose, a world that was a little more innocent. A gentler world where a greater sense of community thrived as people looked out for each other. Those were days when no one ever locked their doors, and life was much simpler and happier. Parents could send their children to school with the relative certainty that they would come home again. It was a time when those sacred boundaries that had marked out the greatest generation had by then not yet been completely removed by the psychedelic counterculture of a new and emerging generation who were desperately searching for a brave new world.

We would be gone all day and return home tired and dishevelled to eat and collapse into bed and fall into the kind of sleep that only belongs to childhood, a sleep we will always yearn to recapture for the rest of our adult lives. Time was stealing away the years right from under our runny noses.

We met at the bus stop. Ten of us were going to the fair. The forty-one bus was supposed to arrive every half hour, but as usual, no bus showed up for two hours, then four turned up at once. That was typical for Lancashire County transport. It was a large red and white double-decker bus. We all piled upstairs. Soon the surly bus conductor ap-

peared, looming over us, with hard, cynical eyes, a rugged
jawline, a beer belly, and a thick moustache; she was not in
any mood for our nonsense. "Fares, please," she barked,
making everyone jump and reach for their pockets. There
was much shuffling and scrambling as we searched for the
sixpences necessary to make the journey. Inevitably, coins
clanked onto the floor and rolled to the front of the bus,
which caused no end of commotion when Ginger crawled
the entire length of the bus through all the other passen-
gers' legs.

Wolfy could not find his sixpence for the longest time.
The conductress had to stand there while he emptied the
contents of his pockets into her hands; these included his
homemade slingshot, two pieces of half-chewed liquorice,
a small tin containing Sid, his giant caterpillar, two rubber
bands, a piece of string, and something indescribable that
made everyone on the bus catch their breath. In the time
it took her to collect our fares, two hundred other passen-
gers had gotten on and off the bus for free.

We had two objectives that day. Our main objective was
to win two goldfish, who would become our den mascots.
However, we also wanted a coconut to eat. They were mod-
est goals, but to us, they were noble pursuits worthy of our
best efforts. Walleyed Mike had been dreaming of winning
glory for himself for weeks. He felt he could win a coconut
on the rifle range. This was where you could shoot at tin
soldiers, and if you knocked them all down with six shots,
a coconut was won. Mike's vision was not the best. The first
inkling that this might not be our most successful attempt
to win a coconut came when he picked up the stall owner's
umbrella and attempted to load it. Eventually, with a deep
sense of trepidation and foreboding, the stall owner gave
him the loaded pellet gun: a semi- automatic, single-shot,

rapid-fire air rifle that fired six metal pellets. The weapon was being fired by a boy who had only moments earlier politely tried to pay the huge, overstuffed teddy bear for his rifle, before the stall owner grabbed his money. What could possibly go wrong?

Sure enough, the stall owner's fears were confirmed when Mikey shot the glass eye out of the furry crocodile on the prizes shelf with his first shot, much to the consternation of the stall owner, who thought better of intervening given the look on Mike's face. The second one pinged off four goldfish bowls in the next stall, which brought cries of alarm from people trying to throw beanbags at a bunch of tin cans. Shots three, four, and five ripped into the stall owner's neatly wrapped lunch pack, shredding the wax paper and burying the projectiles deep into his Spam and cheese sandwich. "That's it!" cried the irate stall owner, who jumped forward to try and grab the gun just as Mike pulled the trigger. The last pellet whizzed over his head, burying itself in the consolation prizes. His assistant managed to grab the rifle, and Mike was disarmed. "How did I do?" Mike asked with a sense of expectation.

"No coconut, Mike," I said, gazing at all the tin soldiers still standing at attention. The stall owner added his angry summary of the incident and given the colour of both his face and language, we thought it best not to ask for the consolation pack of black plastic spiders that now littered the stall and took off.

Next up for us was Beaky on the hoops. These were hoops that had to be thrown over a prize that was on a square plinth block; if that was managed, you won the prize. He had five hoops and very high hopes. Wolfy had disappeared but quickly re-emerged with a long stick. I was not sure where he had gotten it from, but there was a big commotion at the other end of the fair where a tent seemed to have collapsed for no apparent reason. We thought we had done it on Beaky's very first throw when, amazingly, the hoop went over the goldfish bowl, which had two handsome goldfish swimming merrily around. The cheering and excitement were cut short when the stall owner, a rather odd-looking individual with a long face, sticky-out ears, and huge, oversized dentures that were way too white, appeared at the counter before us. He bore a marked resemblance to Mister Ed, the talking horse. He informed us that the hoop had to go over the plinth and the bowl. This caused much consternation, especially with Beaky now remonstrating this most egregious injustice. "Them's the rules," the stall owner kept saying repeatedly, then cussed at us and called us terrible things. Wolfy told him what he could do with his rules and himself, which, though anatomically impossible, was appropriate given the circumstances.

Beaky still had four hoops left. The next three all bounced off the prizes, much to the delight of the stall owner. Then Wolfy whispered something in Beaky's ear, and Beaky threw the last one across toward the back of the stall, which forced the happy stall owner to turn round and pick it up. At that moment, as his back was turned, Wolfy leaned over the small counter and, with the long stick, batted down Beaky's first hoop until it was over the plinth. It became obvious to all at that moment that it would be impossible to do with just a throw. We pointed this out to a perplexed stall owner, who started to say something and then caught himself just in time. Ultimately, he coughed up the bowl and goldfish, and we successfully completed phase one.

We all decided that Wolfy could name our new gang mascots, as his ingenuity had won them in the first place. He was a mad Stingray fan, so it was no surprise that he called them Troy and Marina. We asked him how he knew which of them was Troy. He responded that the one on the left had a cowed look about him, much like his dad did when his mother came into a room, so that was Troy. Next, we needed a coconut!

After the rifle range debacle, we thought throwing darts at cards or small balloons was not such a good idea, nor was the archery stall. Eventually, the plastic horses produced the grand prize for us. One had to throw balls in a hole at the back of the stall; they funnelled back to the front, and the shooter kept throwing. The more balls that got in the hole, the further the player advanced a plastic horse on the back wall, which raced six other horses and competitors. The difficult part was winning two races to get a coconut! Wolfy had no difficulty winning the first one as there was not much opposition: a rather emaciated squib of a boy, a rather dubious-looking individual wearing a bowler hat and a transparent raincoat who threw underhand, and, worst of all, a girl. The second race was different altogether. It produced a shifty teenager who looked like a recovering teddy boy. There was also a round-faced woman with a hat decorated with plastic flowers and a man who looked a lot like the stall owner, possibly a relative who could possibly afford Wolfy some serious opposition.

Wolfy was good, though. He had been throwing rocks at things forever. We often stood on the old railway line, set up tins, and knocked them off with rocks from the top of the embankment. We bombed targets in streams and ponds all the time, sending deserving tins, barrels, and other flotsam to the bottom with extreme prejudice. Once, when Wolfy's action man had lost his foot, it was time to send him to Valhalla. We placed him on my brother's favourite hand-crafted wooden schooner with hand-sewn sails. We doused it all in petrol, set fire to it, and gave the action man a Viking funeral before sinking it with bricks just to make sure he arrived there.

The man looked devious, indeed almost criminal; he was pale of complexion, almost as if he had only eaten porridge all his life like prisoners and Scotsmen. My dad said there was an island off Wales full of desperate people yearning to be free. He had called it Anglesey. According to him, it was a place full of people trying to continually get off the island and come to England to escape compulsory singing and discover vowels. This man had a wild and haunted look about him, as if he had been forced to listen too much to Tom Jones as a boy. Nevertheless, his red plastic horse took an early lead, and all looked lost until Wolfy finally rallied to produce a grandstand finish as his blue horse galloped to victory. He and the coconut were carried shoulder-high around the stall in celebration of his heroic feat.

What was disturbing was that the stall owner had not given us one of the nut-brown, fresh-looking coconuts that he had on display for all to see. He had disappeared into the back, re-emerging sometime later with a dark and seedy-looking object which at some time long ago may or may not have been a coconut. It was balder than my Uncle Albert. It was also thick, dark, and heavy, like my mother's gravy. This coconut looked like it had spent the last twenty years picking up spares on lanes nine, ten, and eleven at the local bowling alley.

Billingsley said things like this had been fired at Frenchmen at the Battle of Waterloo when 'Napolitan Boneyparts' tried to make all of Europe eat snails. It had a menacing look about it. "Let's eat it," said George.

"How are we going to break it open?" said Ginger inquisitively.

"Does anyone have an acetylene torch?" Limpy inquired.

"Funnily enough, I just happen to have one in my back pocket," Wolfy said derisively. "Good, let's eat it," said Big George again, his hunger blinding him to the sarcasm. It was quiet for a few moments; then Beaky had an idea. We would put it under the back wheel of one of the trucks that was about to leave the field, and when it backed up, it would crack the coconut, and we would then eat it. It sounded good in theory. A truck did back over the coconut, but far from cracking, it buried itself in the soft grassy earth. Now, we had to dig it out with sticks. People passing by shouted jovially, "What are you digging for, boys?" "Coconuts," we replied, to which they looked very perplexed and hurried away.

After digging it up and washing it in a puddle, we decided to crack it cricket style by pitching it to Wolfy, who would smack it with a cricket bat we borrowed from a kid who had just won it on the Tombola stall. The coconut would shatter, and we would eat it. Again, the theory was sound. Snowy pitched the coconut, and Wolfy laid on with the bat. Now, there were two things we had not taken into consideration: one was that far from shattering, the coconut would fly off the bat at a frightening speed and elevation; the other thing we had not taken into consideration was the proximity of the parking lot.

The coconut flashed over our heads and into the parking lot. It bounced off several vehicles before popping up right off the windshield of a blue Anglia and disappearing under a Hillman Minx. It was starting to get dark, so we decided to walk home. We walked down the street until we came to a lamppost where Beaky suggested we throw it at the lamppost at point-blank range and see if it broke. Wolfy threw the coconut at the lamppost with all his might but unfortunately missed; it flew over the low brick wall of the house behind the lamppost, bounced twice on the path, and slammed into the front door as if the Dam busters had dropped it. We all ran for cover.

The coconut had ricocheted into the bushes and stayed there. A minute later, the door opened, and a big guy peered out. No one kicked sand in this guy's face, not even Charles Atlas himself. After a while, he returned to the house, so we all crept into the garden and started crawling around, looking for our prize. "Looking for this?" the man said, standing at the gate cutting off our retreat. In his huge hand was our coconut.

We told him the whole story, and he had us all follow him to his garage, where he placed the coconut in a vice, took out a hacksaw, and proceeded to hack it into 10 pieces before sending us on our way. We walked home that evening, eating our coconut with a great sense of accomplishment and well-being. After all, we had achieved our goals, and better still; we had all done it together by pooling our dubious talents and meagre resources.

The Wakes have long since ceased coming to town, and like everything else from those far-off days, they have receded into memory. Almost fifty years later, while visiting family in England, I drove past the old site of the fair, and down the road, we trekked almost half a century before with that obstinate coconut. Outside the house where we were all caught, stood an old man with grey hair, tending his roses. I slowed down and pulled up. Lowering the window, I asked how long he had lived there. "Fifty-seven years," he replied. "Do you ever remember hacking up a coconut?" I asked. He laughed and said, "Were you the mouthy one?" He remembered! The coconut was not the only memorable event in March of 1968, as a couple of weeks later, my mother made a shocking announcement that when acted, upon would be talked about in our neighbourhood for years to come. People still ask each other, were you there that day?

Chapter 11
The Driving Lesson

T he blustery days of March were now blowing themselves out, and those early spring days of 1968 were a time when the innocence of childhood filled the world with all kinds of wonders and marvels that challenged our young imaginations. These mysteries teased our natural curiosity and fostered reckless adventures that shaped and moulded our young lives. We forged lasting friendships that more than stood the test of time. It was a world where a past with no regrets and a future full of hope was held together by an all-consuming present that filled our daily lives with people, places, and moments that only live now in our memories.

Usually, during those lengthening days of late spring, we were out after school building rope swings, constructing dens, or playing sticks in the local stream. Sticks is a nefarious game, especially when played with unscrupulous nine-year-old bookies and their devious sidekicks. The game is simple: you find a stream or a brook somewhere, then choose a stick, preferably something small, sleek, and fast that will easily navigate the currents and eddies of the winding waterway. Then, you all drop your sticks into the water at an appointed place upstream, and the current carries them downstream to the footbridge, which is the finishing line. The first stick to float under the bridge, escaping all hazards and the dead water pools, wins.

This became problematic, though, when Bernard 'Shifty' Blevins started to run a book on all the races, and some of the lads got into hock. Wolfy lost everything on a single race when his stick, which looked like a cert, got hung up mid-stream on something white and unnatural. We later fished the mysterious mass out of the water using Beaky's sister's hockey stick, only to find it was a soggy pair of Y-fronts. How someone's old underwear got into the middle of our stream remains a mystery. There were many suggestions, but the most probable explanation was that someone visiting our town from a nearby port city had decided to do their laundry and became a victim of the current while beating their unmentionables on a rock.

Nevertheless, an adjudicator, who was no less than Big George, was called in because he was seen as neutral. He declared, after much thought and two Curly Wurly's, that though the soggy underpants represented an unnatural hazard, belonging to an unnatural person or persons from unknown regions, he said, tapping his nose knowingly while swigging his Vimto, that it also represented a mutual unnatural hazard, and therefore the result held. Big George's verdict was unpopular but irrevocable, and there was no path to appeal.

Wolfy had lost everything! His brand-new bat-mobile with stick in figures and flaming exhaust pipe, his prized conker with which he had won and held two titles, his collection of Manchester United player cards, two packets of love hearts, two pieces of Bazooka chewing gum, and an Aztec bar that he had foolishly been entrusted to Big George for safe keeping and now no longer remained as an asset to be confiscated. Most of all, he had lost all his marbles, something many of us had suspected for a long time but never outwardly mentioned. He was inconsolable.

To make matters worse, he had lost them to Tricky Smithers, the younger but no less nefarious brother of the infamous slippery Sam Smithers, who was serving six months in Strangeways prison for employing the five-fingered discount at our local store. Having been nabbed, Sam made a run for it. There was a thrilling chase through our village as our local bobbies, Constable Tomkins and Sergeant Patterson, chased him down in their souped-up Anglia. The difference is size between our local police car and the two constables was considerable, so they had to take turns getting in and out of it. Constable Tomkins had to walk back to the station if they arrested someone. Sam had escaped over the fence and ran through all the gardens. Unfortunately for him, it was laundry day, and he got as far as number 13 Balaclava Avenue when he got caught up in a pair of Mrs Howell's oversized bloomers. This caused him to run wildly and blindly into her coal shed and knock himself out on the lintel. When he woke up, Constable Tomkins nicked him. It was a salutary lesson to us all to think that both a man and a boy could lose everything, their whole lives undone by underwear. Constable Tomkins later received the Dixon of Dock Green award for civic duty, which included the 'Evenin All' trophy from the town Mayor for conspicuous gallantry.

That summer, my mother was shocked beyond measure when she caught me reading a book. I had discovered that books had a secondary use besides keeping my bedroom door open and putting them into my brother's backpack when he was not looking to make it even heavier. He was once mystified to find that he had hauled my grandad's large print edition of Roget's Thesaurus, all the way to school with him. Though he had his suspicions, nothing could be proven.

I was reading Robin Hood. This was a guy who robbed the rich to give to the poor. My dad said that was exactly what Harold Wilson was doing. He then got into a terrible mood and disappeared into the garage. I was intrigued by Harold Wilson; he must have been a supervillain who hated England because my dad said that he was destroying the country. Furthermore, his villainous weapon of choice was a pipe. More than once, I had heard my dad talk about taking his pipe and shoving it somewhere. I never knew where, as my mother always interrupted him at that point, and he immediately got angry and went to the shed. As far as I could tell, and according to my dad and what I could pick up from the papers and the BBC, Harold Wilson and his sidekicks Sunny Jim and Roy 'the boy' Jenkins all lived in a formidable fortress called Barbara Castle. From here, they would constantly fight with the opposition at a place called Edward Heath. The journal reveals in its stark and understandable naivety a nine-year-old boy's tentative grasp on politics, which seems in the entries to read more like Eric Morecambe's take on music: "All the right notes, but not necessarily in the right order." My dad seemed to know everything. I was not to come across another fount of knowledge like him until high school, behind the pre-fabs where I learned pretty much everything about the facts of life from Benny Longbanks. For those of us who took the wisdom of the bike sheds as gospel, our future life held more than a few surprises.

I followed my dad into the garage, where he was still muttering about pennies on the pound and taxes. I knew they were bad because the Sheriff of Nottingham had collected these, much to the chagrin of Robin Hood and the great Saxon unwashed. My dad knew lots of things; he called it his sixth sense. I suspected that my mother had a seventh and eighth sense, which was uncanny, as she knew when I had not washed my neck without even looking and sending me back upstairs. She could also find a pair of socks in an empty drawer. She would bang on my older brother's bedroom door as she passed by randomly and shout, "Stop that." She also knew where my dad was on Saturday lunchtime when he went to the hardware store for two hours. I told my mother that the hardware store must be fun because my dad always came back more cheerful than when he left.

My dad also knew when the tooth fairy was coming, except when he and Uncle Albert spent an evening with their mysterious friend Johnny, which they did often. I never saw Johnny, but he was around a lot, and they spoke of him fondly. "What should I call him if I see him?" I once asked Uncle Norman.

"You just call him Mr Walker, but I don't think you will meet him for a while yet." I know my mother did not like Mr Walker. She said he had a very bad influence on everyone. Mr Walker had visited the night I put my tooth under the pillow, and consequently, to my utter dismay, the tooth was still there in the morning instead of a shiny sixpence.

That morning, I was beside myself and immediately approached my dad, who did not look well and kept asking me to speak more quietly. My mother entered the room with a tray, declaring she had brought my dad's breakfast and that he might as well have it in bed. My dad was quite pleased until she placed it on the bed, revealing four aspirins on a large plate along with a teacup full of water. He groaned as she slammed the milk of magnesia down with the words, "That's for dessert." She marched to the door, then turning, looked at her watch, and declared, "Grocery's in half an hour," just to pile on the misery. He looked feeble and forlorn, a broken man, and just for a moment, I thought about postponing my indignant interrogation, but I had to know why that stupid fairy had missed my tooth. He slumped back wearily and scrambled for something at least coherent to fob me off with. He explained that old Mr. Jones on the corner had all his upper teeth removed the same day one of mine fell out. He explained that the tooth fairy had ran out of sixpences, and that the banks were closed because it was Bank Holiday Thursday.

He continued wearily that the fairy, who was not the brightest light in the pixie jar, gave all the sixpences she had to Mr Jones, as he needed them for his meter to keep the electricity on. He added needlessly, in a tone I did not appreciate, that he suspected that the fairy thought Mr Jones' warmth, health, and well-being might be slightly more important than the Mars bar or walnut whip that I would have spent it on. The diatribe continued, his voice getting uncommonly louder as he spoke, declaring that such confectionary would only result in more of my teeth falling out. When I replied excitedly that would mean more money, he collapsed back onto the pillows, looking up at the ceiling and yelling, "I give up." His voice now carried an air of resignation. She had, he said quietly, left me a promissory note on the windowsill downstairs if I was at all doubtful as to her intentions. I ran down to the front room. Sure enough, there it was, with a promise that she would be back with a shilling that night. A whole bob! I told my dad that if she got held up for a few more nights, I would have half a crown by Saturday, to which he responded, "Not bloody likely!" This was not the only time the tooth fairy would prove unreliable.

My mother and father got on very well, and I generally approved of their parenting skills. However, my pocket money had not been raised for a long time, and when it was, it was not index-linked to the cost of living, which was problematic for a nine-year-old with considerable expenses.

All in all, it was a tranquil spring until one morning, my mother made an announcement that nearly brought everything crashing down. She informed my father on Sunday at the breakfast table, just as he was about to smash the top of his boiled egg, that it was high time she learned to drive, that he was to teach her, and that the lessons would begin at once. I knew this was a calamitous announcement because he completely missed his egg and cracked the plate. He then turned very pale, and his hands began to shake. We had to remove the teaspoon from his hands in case he hurt himself. Also, all the birds had suddenly stopped singing outside, and my brother gave out a low whistle, lowered his eyes, and began playing nervously with the saltshaker.

It was not unusual in those days for women of my mother's generation not to drive. None of my aunts drove, nor their friends for that matter. So, this was a remarkable occurrence for a woman of advanced middle years who had been known to have received a caution when in control of a shopping trolly. My father, having recovered his faculties, attempted to reason with her, arguing that she really had no need to drive and that should she change her mind, he, their children, and all humanity would be eternally grateful, and didn't she want the angels in heaven to stop weeping and sing again? My mother declared she did not know what all the fuss was about and that she would have it mastered by the end of the day.

So began what became something akin to the 1962 Cuban missile crisis for our family, and it ended with a photograph that had a good shot of making it into Time magazine.

My dad did at least convince her that learning in my older brother's Morris Minor was the smart thing, and thus only narrowly saved his precious Rover from what he felt was certain destruction. That afternoon, at precisely 1:15 pm, my mother got into the car, and my dad stood there having what for him was the nearest thing to a religious experience. He glared at my mother for several seconds, and at 1:16 pm, she got out of the car and got in on the side where the steering wheel was. His eye roll as she passed him was one for the ages. She reacted with a haughty air of indifference and climbed into the driver's seat.

It was an act attributed only to the kindness of God and his weeping angels that it was a Sunday and that no one was on the road. We lived in a cul-de-sac, so there was at least some temporary protection for human life at one end of the street.

She started the car, and he explained the gears. "What do you mean gears?" she declared. "Doesn't it just go?" His mouth opened two or three times, but nothing came out. She raised her hand and dismissed him with her customary three "Yeses" that I always got. "You can't drive holding your handbag, dear," he said calmly. With the clutch depressed, my mother went at the gear shift like a half-starved wolf at a wounded rabbit. "It must go in one of these," she said determinedly. The unholy sound of grinding, grating, clanking, and screeching was reminiscent of two large armour-clad divisions of cavalry clashing at a great pace on some distant battlefield or my brother's high school brass band warming up for a concert.

It drew everyone within a two-hundred-yard radius to their front window to see where the plane had crashed. She then unexpectedly let the clutch out, and the car lurched forward like a pouncing tiger. I could see my father's head jerk back and forward wildly as the car stopped abruptly. This happened half a dozen times before they reached the end of the cul-de-sac, which was only 50 yards long. It had taken 42 minutes. At that rate, it would have taken them two and a half days to drive around the block.

The car suddenly disappeared around the corner, so we ran after them to follow their progress. There were about fifty people following the jerking automobile up the street. As my mother had yet to pass five miles an hour, the crowd surrounded the car and, peaking in through the open windows, offered encouragement and advice to my mother, and at least one priest on my father's side leaned in to give him the last rights. Then suddenly, she found the accelerator, and the car surged forward, which made everyone gasp as it veered into the opposite lane.

Way up the street, there were numerous cars all backing into each other as they tried to either reverse back up the road or turn around. Men were rushing from their homes to move the parked cars from outside their houses. It had turned into such a mass panic that Mayfield Lane resembled Pamplona during the running of the bulls as terrified men and women signalled to the growing crowds that the fourth driver of the apocalypse was passing the local grocery store.

It was at this point that a good old-fashioned roast beef saved the day. My brother arrived at the car to inform my mother that what was supposed to be our Sunday lunch had now become a black charcoal mass of carbonized flesh adorned with the remnant skins of several potatoes that had launched themselves out of the oven. He claimed he had tried to save our lunch but couldn't find the oven due to the billowing black smoke pouring from the cooker. We all turned and gazed back down the road to see a stream of black smoke swirling up from the direction of our house. My brother informed us that old man Fanshaw, our next-door neighbour had put the fire out and that everything was now under control.

My mother decided to turn the car around and return to the house. The Guinness Book of World Records called us later to confirm that her forty-nine-point turn was indeed a record. It was like a scene from 'Death Race Two Thousand' with people diving for cover in all directions. By the time she was facing the right direction and heading home, she had scored 28 points. My father relieved that they would not spend the early part of the week jerking and hopping around the village, guided her back to our driveway. He then possibly made the worst suggestion ever made in the entire history of the world. He suggested she park it in the garage. Those were words that would come back to haunt him more than once.

They were now at the entrance to the driveway. This time, the clutch caught, and to everyone's surprise, mainly my mother's, the car surged down the driveway. All was going well until my mother asked how you stopped it. "With the brake," said my father very loudly as the garage, whose doors were firmly closed, came ever closer. It was at this point that he dislocated the entirety of his lower extremities, trying to get his leg across the console to find the brake. My mother, shocked by his sudden actions, tried to change gears, jerked the steering wheel wildly, and the vehicle suddenly swerved, missing the garage altogether as it sped down the ever-narrowing garden path. The dustbin was the first to disappear, flying off into Fanshaw's garden with a loud, tinny crash, which scared the Evian out of the feral cats lurking under the porch. She bounced over the lawnmower and my brother's bike, which she was now dragging down the garden path with the undercarriage. Sparks flew everywhere before she eventually careened up the side of the lawn, skirted the length of the privet hedge, scaled the miniature rock wall, and stalled to a dead halt amid my father's prize chrysanthemums.

There was a moment of stunned silence. Then, my mother exited the car as if nothing had happened to voracious applause from the vast and excited crowd. She coolly informed my father that would do for a first lesson. She then waved at everyone packed into the driveway and garden and went inside to repair the dinner and most of the plaster on the pantry wall.

When all the excitement had subsided, and everyone had gone, my father eventually emerged from the car, muttering inaudibly under his breath as he walked jerkily to the house and the phone. Ten minutes later, he left with Uncle Norman to go see Mr Walker for a long and sustained counselling session. The lads came around after our Spam and lettuce dinner was over. Ginger said it was not every day you got to see a Morris Minor with handlebars poking out parked in a bed of yellow chrysanthemums. Grabbing my dad's Polaroid Instamatic that he had received as a gift from my mother the previous Christmas, I snapped the only existing photograph, which sits in my study alongside the silver framed picture of my brother flat on his back on the pebbles of Colwyn Bay beach, completely covered in marauding seagulls.

Despite that photograph of the car resting in the flower bed, my mother always denied it ever happened, and from that day forth, it was never openly talked about again. Despite that warm Sunday afternoon in late March 1968, my parent's marriage survived. They were married for over sixty years. Needless to say, it was the first and last driving lesson my mother ever had!

The remaining days of March passed without incident, and a precarious state of normalcy returned to our household. April arrived with bright sunshine and showers, and though I wasn't to know it then, it was that April that I began a love-hate relationship that would remain with me until this day. It all started when I faced the greatest test of my football career, as I found myself taking a penalty kick against an international goalkeeper with ten bob on the line.

April

Chapter 12

Bolton Wanderers and other Punishments

I t was early April. The clocks had all sprung forward an hour, and the days were lengthening now as the soft and lingering light spread itself in purple hues across the long, dusky evenings. Spring had begun at long last to breathe new life into an emerging world, stretching itself out before us in eager anticipation as we edged toward the long, warm summer yet to come.

I was, of course, no stranger to punishment; it came with the territory of being nine years old. It could come in many forms, of course. Fining, for example. Who among us has not had their pocket money stopped until whatever it was you broke had been paid for? There were time-outs when I had to stand in the corner, usually the corner where the television was, and hold the indoor aerial so I could make myself useful while serving my time. There were also spankings, which were meted out when and wherever necessary. These were usually issued due to sheer bloody-mindedness, like when we rowed on Derwentwater.

My dad was not in a good mood to begin with. While we were on the lake, my mother was in Keswick town centre, engaging in retail therapy with Aunt Hester and my dad's wallet. The only thing that could possibly eclipse the peaceful serenity of this Lakeland haven was the knowledge that my mother was in spending mode. He did not look well when we got in the boat.

In the boat that fateful day, was Uncle Norman, my dad, my brother, my cousin Tom, and me. I knew I had already pushed my father beyond the limits of human endurance by asking him every two minutes if I could row yet. He patiently explained that I was too small and that if he let me take an oar and Uncle Norman continued with the other, we would row in ever-decreasing circles until, as he put it, we would disappear up our own stern. I pointed out defiantly that my brother had been rowing for 20 minutes and had yet to hit the water.

"No," he yelled, but his rebuke only served to harden my resolve as I waited for my chance. If I wasn't going to be given it, then I would take it.

A few minutes later, my cousin Tom was pointing out the tip of Helvellyn in the distance, which was apparently the highest point in England. My brother sat there with a giant smug grin on his face, enjoying my misery. Everybody was standing precariously, trying to see the top of the distant peak when it happened. This was the moment I had waited for, as no one was looking. I lunged for my brother's oar; he stood to defend himself, and the boat rocked wildly. Everyone else was already standing and lost their balance. Uncle Norman tried desperately to correct himself, but it was too late; the boat lurched, and everyone but me and my brother went into the water; the boat then righted itself suddenly, and there went my brother into the water on the other side. My whole family was in Derwent Water Lake, splashing and shouting. I knew I was in for it, but at least I got to row for a bit.

When we all entered the tearoom, my mother and Aunt Hester were already there; I was the only dry one. Everyone in the packed room stared at the men, all soaked and freezing. My mother was not best pleased and forced us to leave through the back door. The spanking, when it came, was equal to the crime. What I appreciated about my father was that he waited until he was no longer mad or wet before administering the punishment. He always refused to discipline in anger.

Not all punishment is visited upon us; some is self-inflicted. Just ask anyone who went to Burnden Park every Saturday to watch Bolton Wanderers play. Sometimes, we cannot help ourselves, such as with car accidents. Some things are so bad that we cannot help watching them.

My unfortunate and self-inflicted love-hate relationship with Bolton Wanderers began in the late spring of 1968 when Simon 'Scowey' Scowcroft invited us to his house for a kick-around on his back lawn, which was huge and had a set of football goals on it. On this Saturday morning, I won the penalty-taking contest. I declared to everyone there how modesty forbade me from telling them how good I really was at taking penalties. It was then that Scowey's brother Kurt declared that I was not as good as I thought I was and declared that I could not even score on his creaky old uncle, let alone anyone else. I took issue and said I would score on any Scowcroft he cared to present. "A bet then," he said, "Shall we say ten shillings!" "Absolutely," I replied, confident that I could beat any pensioner from the penalty spot.

Two weeks later, we all met in his yard for the contest. "Roll him out then, your old uncle, if he's awake," I said.

"Good one," said Wolfy.

"Here he comes now," Scowey replied, and we all looked. Out from the house strode a tall, dark-haired man in a green goalkeeper's shirt, shorts, socks, shoes, and gloves. This was no pensioner, no knock-kneed wobbly old man with grey hair and a stoop; this was Eddie Hopkinson, former England International and Bolton's current number-one goalkeeper.

"He's your uncle?!" I asked as Eddie put on his England cap, which I thought was a bit overkill. Needless to say, it took an England goalkeeper to save my penalty kick I argued later over breakfast with Eddie and the lads. He was a real gentleman and fun for guys to kick around with. Eddie cooked us sausages, and I was hooked. It was all worth the ten bob I lost to Scowey's brother; after all, it isn't every day an England International saves your penalty.

I asked Uncle Albert if he would take me to watch Eddie and Bolton play. He agreed, and I went off every week until I was old enough to go to the games with the lads. Until then, he would take me to the game and then leave me sitting in the stands and disappear just after the kick-off and return two minutes before halftime, staggering down the steps, slumping into his chair and yelling in a slurred manner, "Come on you reds!" At this point, I informed him that Bolton were playing in white. The whistle sounded, and he yelled, "Half time." Then he got up and stumbled up the wooden gangway, telling me we needed refreshment. He returned at the start of the second half, handed me a half-eaten pork pie, passed out in the seat next to me, and snored through the entire second half.

I had become a Wanderers fan, one of the great unwashed that swelled the ranks of the Burnden stand. On one occasion, we were driving to a game. It was a cup match on a Wednesday evening, with my dad at the wheel and Uncle

Norman riding shotgun. A man came running down the centre lane and knocked on the window.

"Are you going to the game?" he said breathlessly.

"Yes, hop in," said my dad, and he climbed in the back with me. That is how I rode to the match with Warwick Rimmer, the Bolton captain. He had gotten caught in traffic, parked his car up, and decided to run to the ground until he saw we were free of the traffic and cadged a lift. We dropped him off, and he was so grateful he made it to the game on time that he asked for my name and address and arranged for me to be a ball boy at Burnden Park.

I knew I was fully hooked on the pain when the Wanderers played Chelsea in the FA Cup one night. The game should have been played at the Little Big Horn because it was such a massacre. It was of course not Bolton's greatest humiliation, that came back in the 1902-3 season when they were so bad that the fans remonstrated with the clubs' governing board about a huge flaw in the construction of the main stand, complaining that it was facing the pitch.

The club's moment of deepest shame, which even now is only whispered of in remote corners, came in a pre-season game during those dark days at the beginning of the 1902 – 1903 season when they were supposed to play Newcastle United in a pre-season friendly at Bolton's ground Burnden Park. The Newcastle bus made a fateful wrong turn on the way down to Bolton, and to everyone's horror, they found themselves in Sunderland. The bus and the team disappeared for three whole days only to reappear with every single Newcastle player refusing to ever speak about what had happened; they did, however, say how much they all needed collective therapy. Had they been taken by aliens and abused, or had they been taken by Sunderland fans and abused? Are Sunderland fans and aliens the same thing as most people believe they are? There were far more questions than answers. No one would ever know.

Being desperate to play a warmup game and having no time to reschedule the fixture, Bolton had to find another team to play against at short notice. The only team available was a circus team that was in town performing that week at the old market in Bradshawgate. The hastily arranged game kicked off at 7:00 pm the next night. A huge crowd was expected as everybody believed Bolton would win the game easily despite the current form of the team. The Bolton evening news covering the game reported that the circus team started four clowns in defence that night, with many believing that was only seven less than Bolton had on the field.

According to the Evening News, Bolton were outfoxed by the Circus eleven's midfield which consisted of right winger Mr Kilowatt, the human dynamo, who, according to the reporter, was simply electric that night. Also, Arthur Byers the illusionist whose performance at centre mid was described by the Evening News as pure magic. Bobby Blanks, the human cannonball, reportedly blasted through the Bolton defence time after time, and the world's least visible man playing left wing ran the Bolton right fullback Charlie Whelan ragged. The paper quoted Whelan as saying after the game, 'I never saw him coming.' In the end, the game was decided after Sid Bricks, the escape artist who, broke free from the midfield, unlocked Bolton's defence, and released the bearded lady who rounded the goalkeeper to score the only goal of the game.

The loss was the blackest day in the club's history. So, that night against Chelsea, when I lost count of how many they had scored, I was reminded that there had been worse days, and because of that, there would be better days, too, and there were. Chelsea got a bag full that night, but it did not matter. Standing there on cold winter nights and Saturday afternoons with my fellow sufferers beneath the floodlights amid the scent of woodbines and Bovril is a memory I will never forget. I know because I have tried very hard, even hypnotherapy, but nothing worked. Despite it all, the memories stay with me because I know they were magical days, the likes of which come only once.

Those days on the terraces with the lads, no matter the score, have left an indelible mark. Every weekend through childhood, adolescence, and even into early adulthood, we assembled in the Lever end to push, shove, sing, and occasionally cheer, come fog, snow, rain, or hale. After all, wasn't this what God made Saturday afternoons for?

Of course, there were times when my punishment was being banned from watching the matches due to some errant behaviour or colossal piece of stupidity, which on one occasion, led to a four-match ban as well as other grave restrictions, all because of a boy's desire for gold.

Chapter 13
Thorndyke's Treasure

———◆◇◆———

As a boy of nine, 1968 was a year of excitement and adventure. By mid-April that year, a lot was going on worldwide. I was not sure where Vietnam was, but it was on the news a lot. I had to decipher the news through the filter of my parents, mainly my dad, whose comments, unfortunately, were beginning to inform my embryonic worldview. I knew that a lot of young people in America, called Hippies (my dad had a lot of other names for them), were very angry and spent a lot of time marching, fighting, and yelling because the American soldiers in Vietnam were also marching, fighting, and yelling. They all had very long hair and beards, from which I concluded they had in their righteous fury killed off all the barbers first.

They also kept sticking two fingers up at the camera. That was a sign I was not allowed to make as my dad said only bad people did this, and if they continued to do it, their fingers would fall off as a result. He said if I had no fingers, I would not be able to pick up a pen or open a book, and therefore, I would not be able to read or write or be productive in the world, and that, consequently, I would have to go live in Wigan. I did not want that, so I never did the sign. He also said that I was not to repeat any of the words I had heard him say while watching the news, especially around my mother, or he would stop my allowance and make me watch 'Panorama' every week for the rest of my life. I had not seen him this agitated since Yugoslavia gave Sandy Shaw no votes in the Eurovision Song Contest.

To calm down, my dad decided to go fishing. He also decided in his infinite wisdom that it was time my brother and I learned to fish. He took us to Farmer Newton's place at the south end of our village cricket field. Here, there were two ponds, which he assured us were full of fish. My brother asked my dad if there would be any piranhas in the pond. My father and I both stared at him for a long time before my father sighed deeply and turned away without responding. "Can we throw him in?" I asked quickly, hoping to capitalise upon the mood of the moment. No, Jimmy, we can't, "Your mother wouldn't like it," he replied sternly. "Everybody else would," I shouted at his receding back.

We arrived at the pond and set up. I was busy watching two maggots race along the back of my hand while my brother had my dad bait his hook. My dad said that when the maggots were cold and lazy on winter days, real fishermen put them in their mouths to warm them up and get them wriggling. "Cool," I said, "let's all do it." I almost got a couple in my mouth before my dad stopped me. My brother recoiled in alarm at the prospect and refused point-blank. Only later, when I spied his half-opened lunch pack containing the sandwiches my mother had prepared for him before we came, that I perceived there might yet be a way to get a maggot or two into his mouth and make a real fisherman of him.

There was a small island in the middle of the pond that was overgrown with weeds and brambles and looked extremely forbidding. My brother was thoroughly absorbed in reading an article on the many shades of beige, so I asked my dad to tell me the story behind the island in the pond. Many famous people have lived in our village, including England football and cricket captains and World Cup winners. In my teens, I recall being stuck in Mrs Allen's shop, waiting for the bread man to unload his van. Stuck in the shop with me that day was Frank Worthington, an incredibly gifted player and renowned playboy who lived in our village. We talked for a good fifteen minutes about his life and his time at Bolton, but that conversation is for a later book. I recommended he try the whole grain artisan loaf, which he did. I do believe that his game improved shortly after our meeting. It could have been the bread.

Thinking back now, that conversation with Frank and including being Alan Ball's paperboy, my contribution to British football seems to have been more significant than I first thought. In fact, if any village in Britain could field a five-a-side team consisting of anyone who had ever lived in that village, ours would be formidable. Our village team would include the most decorated Premier League player in history, two of the most famous players ever to play the game, and a multiple Ballon d'Or winner, along with our very own World Cup winner. It wouldn't be a bad team. Plus, Kenneth Wolstenholme could commentate for us. I like to think I would have at least made the bench. However, one of the most famous men of our village was old Doc Thorndyke. Doc lived in the village in the 1640s when Charles I was on the throne, and Bolton Wanderers had last won the FA Cup.

Local legend had it that Charles was short of gold to fight the civil war raging across England and had sent word to Scotland that he needed money. Upon hearing Charles' need for money and that a collection was to be taken up, the population of Scotland suddenly shrank from three million to ninety thousand. That small remnant of Scots comprised the entire inhabitants of a wee village at the foot of Loch Dour, who had not heard of the levy due to a matter of fighting the English at the Battle of Hampden Park. Consequently, they were relieved of their gold, and upon taking the tax back to Oxford, the platoon of Cavaliers entrusted to deliver it was set upon by a bunch of roundheads while traveling through our village.

All the roundheads who had stolen the gold were hunted down by the Royalists, until the last one came to old Doc Thorndyke, the village physician, and asked him to hide it for the sake of the cause. He agreed and initially hid it at the bottom of a barrel of leeches he had borrowed from the Inland Revenue Service that he used to heal the sick and infirm. Later, after the old Doc succumbed to an overabundance of strong ale and bad women, or was it bad ale and strong women? This was never clear; the barrel was eventually emptied, but there was no gold. The only clue was that he had been seen swimming here in the pond late at night, only a few days prior to his demise. Was he searching for more leeches? Had a strong woman pushed him into the pond after drinking bad ale, or was he hiding the gold on the island as was suspected? Nobody knew, and the gold was never found. My dad said that most villagers believed it was buried on the island.

I was captivated by the prospect of finding hidden gold and relayed the story to the lads, who immediately wanted to go dig it up. So, a plan was formed. This would be tricky as the pond was on Old Farmer Newton's property. We all knew that Farmer Newton only loved three things: Old Mrs. Farmer Newton, distilling manure into liquid form, and shooting small boys with salt pellets when they snuck onto his land without his permission. It would take a cunning plan to ensure our safe capture of the gold, which would require all of Beaky's limited intelligence.

Beaky was the smartest one of us all. He had mastered addition, could tie his shoelaces, and once received a Blue Peter Badge for saving a nest of Robin's eggs from council workmen who were about to chop down the tree. Beaky had climbed the tree, rescued the eggs, and was on his way down when he slipped off the branch and fell, hitting almost every branch. He had received the badge from the late great Sir John Noakes, who can be seen in a photo on Beaky's mother's sideboard. In the picture, Noakes can clearly be seen presenting the badge to a scratched-up and severely bandaged dwarf who looked like Tutankhamun's younger, smaller, and less fortunate brother.

Nevertheless, it made Beaky a true hero. Beaky concluded that we must build a raft and sail it to the island at dawn while old Farmer Newton was in bed, hopefully with Old Mrs Farmer Newton. "What about his two dogs, Blinky and Ethel?" asked Wolfy. This was a good question. "Nothing to worry about," said Limpy, "Blinky is as blind as a bat." "He once stood barking at a wooden post that had a workman's hat on it for 12 hours before he realised it wasn't human, then he trotted off and fell in a ditch." "Ethel never leaves the kitchen in case she misses some food." He continued his report on Ethel, the dog, stating that she had no mobility; he went on, as she had eaten so many scraps and became so wide that the Newtons used her as an auxiliary coffee table with ears. This was comforting as the last thing we needed was barking dogs alerting everyone within ten square miles to our covert operation.

We first needed a raft to get us to the island. A rubber dinghy was suggested but discarded on account of wearing out all our lips blowing it up. Frothy remarked on our dismal performance at Ticker Turner's birthday party when we were given the job of blowing up the balloons. At the end of a frenetic hour of huffing and puffing, we had managed one half-inflated green balloon that looked more like an overgrown lime, after which we all had to take a nap.

So, we set about building a raft with fence posts from behind Wolfy's dad's garage and some sheetrock from a place better left undisclosed even now. With a few lusty blows of the hammer, some wire, and string, she was ready to be launched. At first sight, the 'Cynthia Louise' did not look like other boats and did not inspire one with confidence, lolling lopsidedly in the water. One felt the disturbing sense that she had more of the feel of a Lusitania or Titanic than a Victory or a Golden Hind.

She would hold four brave souls: Me, Wolfy, Mikey, and Ginger. We boarded her very carefully, considering we had both a pick and a shovel borrowed from Beaky's dad. We were to paddle over to the island using the shovel and a wide piece of particle board improvised into an oar. We started paddling. There was much splashing and shouting and grunting and thrashing with the odd word that would have sent me straight to the front room if I had uttered it in our house. After a few minutes, exhaustion set in, and the frenetic activity gradually died down, and we lay there panting. "Might be easier if you let me untie the raft first?" said Beaky, in a tone of resigned irony. This time, we glided off seamlessly across the glassy pond.

Dawn was just breaking, and the first olive moments of daylight raised our spirits as we surrendered ourselves to a tranquil morning on a smooth pond. Plan A was to row both there and back, but we also had an ingenious plan B. Beaky had tied a rope to the raft. In an emergency, we would blow the little airhorn we had with us, and the guys would yank on the rope, and we would all come speeding back faster than Donald Campbell on Coniston water.

We were off to find Thorndyke's treasure and become rich beyond our wildest dreams, richer than Algernon Prim, or Primmy as he was known, who lived at the end of our road. We all envied and disliked him, as he always had the latest and greatest of everything. If you had a pop gun, he had a Johnny Seven. If you got a new bike, the next day, he had a Chopper. If you got a puppy, he got a lion cub.

We had all sat around the previous evening discussing what we would do with our share of the loot. Beaky said he would buy a new chemistry set and a new garden shed for his dad, as they were both unfortunately destroyed in a mysterious explosion. Wolfy said he would buy a bottle of Vimto that refilled automatically; he also wanted a kiss from Henrietta Pross. "The Medusa," said Mikey, using her nickname, "She will turn you to stone." Jingo wanted a sister. We enlightened him by pointing out to him that you do not buy sisters, informing him that the government gives them to your parents when you are not looking. I said I had seen a place on 'Zoo Time' where Johnny Morris said they trained chimps in human behaviour. Even the most stubborn and stupid ones learned basic functions, so I thought there might be an outside chance there was a place for my brother, no matter how much it cost. We all agreed that we would buy our school and close it down so that we could just play out every day like the summer holidays. Also, we would buy a mountain of Mars bars and eat our way to the summit.

Here we were, on the verge of realising all our dreams. We stepped onto the island, but the undergrowth was too thick to reach the centre. We could not see anything, and there was the rhythmic hum of what sounded like a motor, but we paid no heed to it. We were going to be rich! We scouted the edge of the island until we found an open space. This must be it, as it was the perfect place to bury treasure, and it must be the place as there was a stake at the spot with a red tie on it. Obviously, it was left there by the old Doc so he could remember where the booty was buried. "Dig here," said Wolfy, and we started in. We dug down a couple of feet until we heard a 'chink.' Surely, this must be the box. "Pass me the pickaxe!" yelled Ginger. This was not really a phrase that any sane person would want to hear coming from us, as usually, the result of any request of this ilk would invariably end in disaster; this time was no different. "I am not sure," but my sentence went unfinished as Ginger swung down with the tool. What happened next was and still is all a bit of a blur.

There was a tremendous hissing noise, then a large gushing sound and a huge black mass of liquid came flying up into the air, showering us with mud and sludge. Our first reaction, as it always was when presented with something we knew was not right, was to run, so we ran. There were faint images of geysers, lots of running, yelling, and jumping, the loud sound of an air horn, dogs barking, a tightening of the rope, the rapid movement of a raft, a momentary sense of flight, then water!

By the time Old Farmer Newton's truck arrived, we had managed to swim to the raft and had been pulled ashore. Blinky and Ethel were barking; they did not know what at, but they were barking all the same. Old Farmer Newton was yelling at us, and we stood there, all ten of us, four of us soaked, bedraggled, and shivering. It was then that we heard it. Of all the sounds one hears in one's lifetime: your mother singing, your brother coming down the hall after finding his bed missing, or your cat being run over by the coal wagon. Not even the fateful wail of a crowd being forced to watch Bolton Wanderers play at home, non-prompted a change of underwear more than this, a siren, and the police.

This meant parents, which meant an uncertain future, if there was one at all. This would be no mere perp walk into the front room; this meant the end of life as we knew it. Man would live on Mars, cars would fly, wars would cease, and Bolton would have won an away game by the time I saw the light of day again. All because of gold. Such is the piteous nature of the human condition. I would like to say that Sergeant Steele only reprimanded us, boxed our ears, and sent us off tails firmly between legs, but 'Oh no,' we each had to call our parents and have them come and get us from Old Farmer Newton's house. At least there was a fire, as we were freezing, and Old Mrs. Farmer Newton was very kind, giving us all hot chocolate while repeating, "What were you boys thinking?" every two minutes.

What made matters worse was it was only 7:00 am on a Saturday morning, the day our parents slept in. We all sat there in stony silence, waiting to be taken away in turn. Old Farmer Newton and police Sergeant Steele gazed out of the window at the fountain of water still shooting out of the island, like a Texas gusher in need of Red Adair. One by one, we were all taken away by irate parents who all apologised profusely to Old Farmer Newton and Sergeant Steele. We were not to be prosecuted, but Sergeant Steele expected our parents to exact upon us the necessary retribution.

My dad explained it to me every weekend for the next four weeks as he sat in his deck chair, watching me carry and clean every brick for his new garage. He explained that Old Farmer Newton used the island as a pumping station to irrigate his fields, and we dug into his main pressure pipe. Thus, our fountain would not have been out of place at some sewage version of Versailles. He said it was very serious and expensive, and he and the other dads had had to pay for it. I wondered why my dad was out in the yard with me for the first two weekends. I later learned my mother had taken a dim view of him telling me stories. "There is enough nonsense in his head already without you adding to it with tales of gold," she said. He had pitifully tried to defend himself, but our colossal idiocy had somewhat eclipsed his "feeble excuses. "The gang was not permanently finished, though, and in time, our parents' wrath abated, and life returned to normal. The island remains, to this day, in the pond at the back of the cricket ground, and even though Old Farmer Newton and Sergeant Steele are both sadly long gone, I believe the gold is still there, just waiting for another attempt!

It would be four weeks before I saw the light of day, but eventually, everything returned to normal, and I was allowed out again. I couldn't have guessed that my first weekend of freedom would be spent in a place I would rather not have been, simply because I would have to spend a whole weekend in a haunted house.

May

Chapter 14
The Ghost of Walmsley Manor

———◦———

A fter the debacle on Farmer Newton Pond and our disastrous attempt at treasure hunting, my four-week incarceration came to an end, and I was allowed out into the world once more. By now, it was mid-May, and the cherry blossoms were in full bloom, and the days were warm. I was only allowed out with my Parents during my incarceration, which happened the first week when we went to buy some new football boots. We were off to Timpson's at the top of Westfield Road. I had wanted a pair of Hummels or Adidas, but all I got was a pair of Timpson toe bungers. These were all black with red laces, and even though not worn by Pele, they were actually quite stylish for a nine-year-old on the village green.

My second week of penal servitude was spent trying to work out why the plastic tip of the laces on the left side of the boot barely poked through the last hole at the top while on the right side, the lace was 14 feet long. Try as I might, threading and rethreading, it always came out the same. I tried to wear them this way by wrapping the long lace around my boot eight times, around the top of my socks, and then up through my shorts, around my waist twice, under my shirt, and out at the top where I cello taped the plasticky bit to my collar. These attempts to lace my boots preoccupied me for another three weeks until I accidentally managed to balance them in a moment that almost ascended to a religious experience. By then, I had served my time.

However, my first weekend of freedom was not what I had planned. Wolfy had been invited to spend the weekend at their family estate in Cheshire. With the exception of Wolfy's and Beaky's dad, the journal entries' only other mention of any of the lad's relatives is Wolfy's Uncle Harry and his cousin Bobby. The estate had been in the family for generations and was now run by Wolfy's Uncle Harry, who by all accounts was a bit eccentric and a recluse. The invitation had been extended to one friend, and that friend was me. My brother let out a long whistle and grimaced in his usual way. "You're going to Walmsley Manor?" he said when I told my mother I had been invited. "Walmsley Manor for the weekend?" he continued, shaking his head. Somehow, I just knew what his next words were going to be, and I said them with him, "It's haunted," we said in unison. "No, it really is," he said as he began to tell us the story of Lord Harwood, the first Duke of Malahide, and his young and beautiful wife, and what can happen if you're not careful with envelopes.

"One fateful day," my brother began, "the duke's wife had written two notes, one to her husband, the duke, and the other to the milkman, who had been doing less than a stellar job. She had sadly put the notes in the wrong envelopes. The milkman had received a note informing him of how much she enjoyed seeing him first thing every morning, how much she appreciated all that he brought to her, and how much she loved and adored him and yearned to bear his children." Her husband, however, the duke, received a note informing him that the current arrangement was most unsatisfactory, and after years of the usual, she was now considering getting sterilized. Furthermore, she did not like all the noise he made so early in the morning and the way he flirted with the under-house parlor maids at the back door. Consequently, she declared she no longer required his services and would try George, the village grocer, instead. Immediately upon receiving the note, the duke went up the grand tower and threw himself off, killing himself and three dozen marigolds that had just been planted in the east flowerbed."

I had a long acquaintance with my brother's cheap theatricals and concluded that he was trying to scare me, but this time, he had no success whatsoever. Well, not until the next day. The following day, Aunt Kathy came around because my mother was experiencing a sudden and unnatural dalliance with her appearance, indicating the possibility of a midlife crisis. She had, on a whim, decided to go two shades lighter on her hair colour, which had resulted in many midnight phone calls, meetings, and deliberations with her friends and, above all, with Aunt Kathy, her hairdresser, who had come around to discuss the new rinse. After it was all decided, my mother excitedly announced the news about her hair to my dad over dinner. His response of, "Very nice dear, I will alert the local news when I have finished my chops," was not the response she had hoped for, and consequently, my dad had great difficulty finding his dessert.

Aunt Kathy was not my real aunt. It was funny how women of a certain age who were friends of my parents required me to call them Aunt. I had forty-one in all. This worked well on birthdays and visits when they insisted on giving me money. I had once determined that if each of my aunts gave me five pounds a year for the next three years, and my parents lived until they were a hundred and ten, I could take early retirement when I was twelve.

My mother had mentioned my going to Walmsley Manor to Aunt Kathy, who responded, "Rather him than me, it's haunted, you know, oh yeah." She went on sloshing away loudly on her Wrigley's Juicy Fruit as she told the exact same story my brother had told about dukes, letters, milkmen, and crushed marigolds.

"What was that?" Aunt Kathy asked as the door slammed behind me. I was on my bike up to Wolfy's faster than our dog had scarfed down my dad's dessert the previous evening. Wolfy was in the garden when I arrived, leaning over the side of the garden pond, scaring the goldfish. "I heard your Uncle Harry's place is haunted," I said breathlessly.

"That's right," he replied nonchalantly.

"What!?" I replied. On the ride-up, concern had given way to panic, but now hysteria was raising its ugly head. I had to think fast. "I think I am coming down with something," I said, possibly the plague." Feel my head. It's all hot and sticky, and my pulse is five hundred beats a minute. I don't think I can come on Friday."

"Jimmy, you just rode here uphill all the way; of course, your sweating, and your pulse is fast," Wolfy replied. He continued, "You might be right, though; it could be jaundice," he commented sarcastically. "You do seem to be turning yellow." There was no need for that, I thought, and immediately realized that word of my cravenness would get out, and I would be branded a coward and have to travel the earth for the rest of my life trying to prove myself brave like Chuck Connors in Branded. If Cynthia Hardcastle should hear of my funk, then it would be too hard to bear, ghost or no ghost.

So, it was late one evening in May 1968 that we found ourselves at Wolfy's Uncle Harry's house. Wolfy's dad had dropped us at the gate and not the house, which wasn't overly reassuring. The driveway was long and winding, and the night was drawing in. Deep dark shadows framed the barren trees that lined the gravel pathway as we strolled toward the house.

"What do we do if he appears?" I asked.

"Who?" replied Wolfy.

"You know, Lord Hedgerow, the Duke of Marmalade. What happens if he appears?"

"We run," said Wolfy rather too casually.

"You can't outrun a ghost," I said,

"Really, watch me," he replied with conviction.

Eventually, we came to the house, which stood on twenty acres of land. It had two small towers with cone-shaped turrets on either side of the large and disjointed house. There was no light visible anywhere. We knocked, and the door opened. It was Uncle Harry—well, I hoped it was. It was hard to see as the night had drawn in upon us. Inside, the house was very dark, lit only by candles and paraffin lamps.

"Is there a miner's strike on?" I asked Wolfy, looking around the dimly lit rooms. I thought that this might be a power cut.

"He likes to save money," Wolfy informed me.

The hallway was large, with a circular staircase at one end. The living room had a large table that stood by a huge bay window from which long, worn velvet drapes hung down, and there was a fireplace and two armchairs. I looked for Miss Haversham but couldn't see her anywhere, so we sat down. A small television sat in the corner; Captain Pugwash was on, but there was no sound. If Robert Louis Stevenson, Charles Dickens, and Edgar Allen Poe were to share a house, then this would be it. I was surprised that only one ghost hung out here.

"You boys must be hungry," Uncle Harry said enthusiastically. It was a statement that could never ever be contradicted. Uncle Harry looked like Wolfy, except bigger. He disappeared into what must have been the kitchen and returned carrying three plates.

"Oh boy," I thought, "Porridge or some Scottish gruel designed to bring on early puberty." In fact, it was fish and chips.

"I got these just before you arrived," he told us. There was Vimto, too. This was awesome. We ate dinner and watched TV until the big grandfather clock in the hall chimed eight and scared the birds out of the eves. "Bedtime," announced Uncle Harry. "You boys are in the long room on the first floor. William here knows the way, and oh, Bobby's coming later," he said and then disappeared. "William, who is that?" I asked.

"Me, dummy," said Wolfy.

"Oh yeah." In harmony with the evening, Uncle Harry said goodnight and went down into the basement, holding his bowl in one hand and a candle in the other, like a scene from Kidnapped.

"He likes to sleep down there," Wolfy informed me. "There used to be a lodger, but he left." "Was it Vincent Price?" I asked as we walked into the dimly lit hall. "He's down there, and we are up here," I inquired. "What happens if there is a fire, a burst pipe, or nuclear war?" I asked, not mentioning the ghost.

The long room was very aptly named. By the time you had turned the light off and walked back to bed, you were exhausted. Wolfy and I decided it was best if we had something to defend ourselves with if the duke should come calling, so we went downstairs in our jammies, searching for a weapon. The only thing we could find was a gaudy old sword.

"I don't think a sword is going to work; you can't stab a ghost," Wolfy said. I was shocked as this made sense, "We need a gun," he said, and as suddenly as it had come, that brief moment of lucidity passed into history. There was no gun, so we took the cheap fake sword back to our room. I knew it was fake because my dad had one in our front room exactly like it. Made in Taiwan, sold in Spain. It had glittering gems of blue and red on the hilt, all made from paste. Our sword had a secret history, though, which wasn't so secret after I had hidden behind the couch one night when my dad recounted the story to Uncle Norman.

The story of the sword was so infamous that my mother had forbidden its telling. Apparently, one warm and languid night in Benidorm, a contingent of Britishers were together in the hotel bar. The night was advanced, and the party was feeling no pain. Compelled to sing after a few bevies as the Brits are disposed to do, they were on their third chorus of the song, 'Torremolinos, Torremolinos', when a group of Germans began singing 'Uno Paloma Blanca' in Teutonic chorus in an attempt to drown out the Brits. My mother rallied the troops. Fuelled by copious amounts of sangria and memories of the Blitz, she climbed up on the table to rouse the British to even greater volume. Being drowned out, the Germans decided more beer was the better part of valour and withdrew. All ended well as both parties were brought together by that legendary statesman and peacemaker, Al Martino, as they all sang 'Spanish Eyes' before staggering off to bed. My dad said that one of the hotel waiters was so moved by the incident that he had fallen madly in love with my mother and presented her with the cheap sword that stood by the fire in our front room. My dad said he was delighted with the amorous waiter, who had, at one stroke, both improved my mother's disposition and their table service.

Armed then with a fake sword, we headed to bed and fell asleep. Later in the night, we were both awakened by footsteps coming up the stairs. "It's him," I said. Go out and look."

"Why me?" answered Wolfy.

"All right, we will both go." I knew I didn't have to outrun the duke; I just had to outrun Wolfy, and I could easily do that, hence the suggestion. We went out into the corridor, and suddenly, the sound of footsteps started again on the stairs, this time coming down toward us. I thought I could smell the faint odour of marmalade. "It's him!" Wolfy cried. "Where's the sword?" "I forgot it", I cried in alarm. Then, a voice came out of the darkness, "William?" It was worse than I thought, the duke knew our names, we were done for. "What are you two boys doing?" the voice asked, turning the corner, torch in hand. Much to our relief, it was only Uncle Harry.

"We heard something," we said a little breathlessly.

"It's just me. Bobby's here," he said jovially. Now back to bed with you." I asked Wolfy about Bobby. Bobby's my cousin," he said, falling asleep. Wolfy's cousin, who probably looked like him too, was a ghastly thought to go to sleep on—another Wolfy.

I sat at breakfast and just stared. "That's Bobby?" I asked Wolfy again.

"How many times are you going to ask me that?" Wolfy said, irritation now replacing exasperation in his voice. Uncle Harry came in with more bacon. "You had better close your mouth before a bird builds a nest in it," he said, putting more rashers on my plate. I was staring at Bobby, sitting across from me, reading the paper. Uncle Harry and Wolfy had been staring at me in awkward silence for some time before Wolfy asked me why I was drinking out of the milk jug and how much jam I was going to smear on that coaster. "That's Bobby?" I repeated,

"Yes," hissed Wolfy.

"That's your cousin?" I went on.

"Yes!" he said.

"By blood?" I continued.

"What is wrong with you?" he demanded, but I did not reply. I was too busy staring at one of the most beautiful creatures God had ever created, and it was a girl! Cynthia Hardcastle's standing as a goddess had now seriously come into question for the first time.

Bobby, or Roberta, was simply stunning. She was eighteen and headed for university that summer. "She is going to Cambridge," Wolfy said. I looked at her, then back at him, then back at her. It was a complete mystery, one of those genetic anomalies that life creates every billion years or so. "And she is related to you?" I asked again, this time with too much incredulity in my voice. There was a limit to Wolfy's tolerance; he was beginning to glare at me. I had seen that glare many times before with other people, and it signified danger. There was a limit to Wolfy's patience, beyond which there was only darkness. I needed to calmly back away from the edge.

Roberta was a lot of fun. She was tall, slim, elegant, with supermodel looks, and a great sense of humour. She was also wonderfully kind. Roberta also drove a fire engine red Triumph Spitfire. I was in love! She borrowed her Uncle's Land Rover and spent the weekend ferrying us around. We went to the movies to see the Disney version of 'Jungle Book.'

After watching the 'Jungle Book' it was late afternoon and Bobby decided we needed to see Blackpool, home of that great British hero George Formby and his little stick of Blackpool rock. The beach proved to be exciting. When on the donkey rides, one of the beasts, seeing his last chance of life on the open range, suddenly went rogue. Unfortunately, he had a pensioner on him at the time. There was much yelling and shouting, with cries of, "Reign him in, Fred!" and "Ride him, cowboy," as the donkey was now reaching a speed nearing two miles an hour. Eventually, the emergency brake was applied, which was a rope tied to the other seventeen donkeys, which saved the day. The pensioner dismounted to much applause, having corralled and tamed the almost runaway beast.

We saw the famous Blackpool Tower and ate all kinds of strange crustaceans and marine life. Wolfy lost his whole carton of mixed mussels and whelks on the super cyclone

at the amusement park, which was very alarming, especially for the lady who later found them in her handbag.

There were crowds of boys around Bobby everywhere we
went, so we didn't have to pay for one ride at the amusement park all night. We arrived back at Uncle Harry's after eating a fish and chips supper. This was very exciting
because we saw the soccer results on the grease-stained
paper, and Bolton somehow accidentally managed to win
against Huddersfield. At first, I thought the paper might
have come from a museum, but no, there was today's date.
It was a glorious day that would live long in my memory.

The duke never did show up, and Wolfy and I spent a
memorable weekend at Walmsley Hall with Uncle Harry
and Cousin Bobby. I asked Uncle Harry if he had ever seen
the duke. "No, I have never seen him," he said, but he
went on sensing our disappointment. "Every year in the
spring," he said in a slow and hesitant voice that hinted
at perplexity, "Yes," Wolfy and I said in unison, eyebrows
raised in rapt attention. "Three dozen marigolds grow in
perfect symmetry beneath the east tower." "That could
just happen naturally," I said with undisguised scepticism.
"Really," replied Uncle Harry, gazing at us intently as he
continued, "Tell me how," he spoke softly, "We had the
whole area paved twenty years ago!" I was in mid-sprint for
the front door when Bobby came into the room to inform
us that Wolfy's parents would be late picking us up, so
Bobby offered to drop me off on her way home. Finally, I
would get to ride in the Spitfire. It was late fall, but she put
the hood down, and we sang "The Bare Necessities of Life"
from The Jungle Book all the way home.

When we got home, my parents weren't back yet, and
my brother was sitting around with his friends; they were
hanging out in the front yard. Bobby drove the Triumph

Spitfire convertible up the drive and stopped in front of them. She got out and grabbed my bag. My brother and his friends were wide-eyed, open-mouthed, and speechless. I could hear gasps and low whistles. The moment was not lost on Bobby, who gave me my bag, bent down, and kissed me on the cheek. "Thanks for a wonderful weekend," she said loudly, winking at me. With that, she straightened up, tossed her long flowing auburn hair, which, for a brief and glorious moment, caught and flashed crimson red in the light of the setting sun, and like a mirage stepping from the glossy pages of Vogue magazine, she strode to her sports car and disappeared from my life forever. All she left behind was the indelible memory of a vision so lovely that it stayed in the deep recesses of my mind for many years. After her tail lights disappeared, I gazed around at all the cod fish, mouths gaping and eyes rolling, and nodded at them calmly. I picked up my bag and sauntered inside with a smile equal to that of the Blackpool Illuminations. It truly was a perfect day.

Uncle Harry is no longer with us, and Walmsley Hall is also gone (it is now a Tesco car park), and with it, the duke, who we never did get to see. Bobby graduated with a first from Cambridge and modelled for several years before becoming a very accomplished solicitor. It was a grand weekend. Years later, and deep into my midlife crisis, I bought a Spitfire just for fun and drove it for a few years. Those days in May live now only in my memory. There were no photographs, and I never saw Bobby again, but the memory of her beauty, grace, and kindness to a nine-year-old boy still lives on in the man he became.

June

Chapter 15
Love and other Yuk

———◆◇◆———

The Whitsuntide holidays were taken in the first week of June that year. The first warm winds of summer had begun to usher out the late spring showers, and the sad, grey morning skies that persisted throughout May were now as blue as robin's eggs. It was on one of those picture-perfect mornings in the early summer that we set out on our mid-term holiday to South Wales.

As can be imagined, the journal entries are not overflowing with moral messages or social and ethical profundity. However, one or two of the entries come very close, as here, describing the half-term holiday week in June 1968, it would seem that my value system shifted at least once during that year. Julie was a rather odd-looking girl who might well have saved my life that week. Until Julie, I confess I was a rather shallow and feckless boy who went for the lookers like Cynthia Hardcastle and Bobby, who between them had captivated me, half of our school, most of the boys in our neighbourhood, my brother, my brother's friends, and half of Blackpool. My somewhat disingenuous and superficial attitude toward the fairer sex changed dramatically after Julie intervened in a rather ugly incident that involved me, my brother, and both his fists.

Women, of course, were banned from the den, and any member of our gang caught associating with them was immediately censured. They weren't even allowed to be mentioned by name in our Sanctus Sanctorum. If this rule were violated, it could result in the most severe punishment. Liking Cynthia Hardcastle was tolerated because every boy in school had secret designs on her one day becoming their girlfriend, later fiancée, and possibly future wife, just as soon as they learned to fasten their shoelaces and began wearing long trousers.

The particularly sordid incident I referred to earlier occurred during our annual family holiday in Wales. We went to Wales because my parents considered it a foreign country, even though it was only 50 miles away. Wales has been a part of the United Kingdom for centuries but still retains much of its ancient ethnic identity, such as its own language. English people often try to learn this language at their own peril.

The Welsh language has an overabundance of consonants and very few vowels. Attempts from non-natives to articulate the words and place names usually result in prolonged paralysis of the larynx, months of therapy, and frequent surgery. On one occasion, I thought my brother had mastered the Welsh language, but it turned out he was choking on a half-masticated piece of Welsh lamb. Everyone was hitting him in an attempt to dislodge the offending food, so I joined in until my mother informed me tersely that slapping him in the face wasn't helping, and much to my chagrin, I had to stop. It was very gratifying when, eventually, the recalcitrant piece of meat was dislodged, and he stopped being blue and returned to his normal pale and insipid self, except for one side of his face, which was a glorious shade of handprint red.

It was off to Wales again for a family trip in the early summer of 1968. It was usually a fun affair. My mother, of course, took charge of the packing. Looking at my dad's

Rover stuffed with everything five families would need for a vacation; it was hard to see where everyone would sit. I couldn't help thinking that if my boyhood hero, Captain Scott of the Antarctic, had had my mother along with him when he set off to discover the South Pole, they would all not only have survived the expedition instead of dying due to lack of supplies but would have returned warm and well fed. Of course, they would have needed a dozen more sleds. They certainly would not have lacked for socks.

"Are you sure we haven't forgotten anything, the freezer or the old wardrobe?" my brother said sarcastically. This prompted my mother to start thinking and my dad to accelerate away from the house before she could remember something else, which, of course, wasn't possible as we had what seemed to be the entire contents of the house crammed into the car. We looked a lot like the Beverly Hillbillies departing for Hollywood. My dad gave my brother that look that I loved so much, the one that would make me an only child if he were to utter another word. He never did, of course, and I had to bear the disappointment once again.

Four hours later, we were deep in Wales and lost. My mother was navigating, which said it all. "It's a wonder we aren't in Scotland," my brother muttered, which summed it all up. Eventually, my dad stopped at a local pub and asked for directions, something he had never done before, but four hours of my mother's navigating forced his hand. Eventually, he came out smelling of Bass Charrington's best pale ale, which my mother immediately jumped upon. He explained he had had to win their favour by accepting their hospitality; my mother was less than convinced. Apparently, the locals had informed my father that we had missed the turn at Phwthwphylllypthw and that we then needed to go straight on to Brysryhpthlcndwnny-cmthylllwynprmthn, down through Llgrygnchlyrrgchrinch until we came to the Tenby bypass, and then on to our destination. "It's all very simple, really," he said. Eventually, more by luck than good management, we arrived in Tenby and settled into our rooms at the Geronwyit Hotel.

It was not just because of the beating I would receive that I remember that infamous day. We spent the day at the beach. I had gone crabbing with my dad in the tide pools while my brother sat with my mother on rented deckchairs. A blanket was spread on the sand, and the old radio was playing the latest chart-topper by Engelbert Humperdinck. Beside my mother were shopping bags full of sandwiches, crisps, scotch eggs, and an assortment of fizzy drinks for when we got hungry.

I built sandcastles surrounded by saltwater moats for hours while my parents read and sunbathed. My brother sat there adjusting his blazer and tie and rolling up his trousers in case he got caught by the tide. He was very excited as he waited for the latest weather forecast to come on the radio. I stood there with my bucket, spade, and the remnants of at least three ninety-nine ice cream cones, complete with chocolate flake and raspberry sauce, around my mouth and down my T-shirt. "Anyone want to bury me?" I asked. My brother leaped to volunteer but was shut down sharply after a rebuke from my mother. He sat back disappointed and continued adjusting his cap as my dad heaped sand upon me.

That night, back at the hotel, when we came down to dinner, I knew something was amok when my mother took out her loathsome hanky, licked it, and started scrubbing my face and ears. I squirmed free and headed for the hotel dining room. It was then that I discovered, to my horror, it was my parents' twenty-fifth wedding anniversary. We entered the dining room, and there was a huge bouquet of flowers and a bottle of champagne on our table. To make matters worse, the rest of the guests began to applaud as they had been apprised of the occasion by the head waiter, who was even now oiling his way across the floor. This was when you wanted the ground to open and swallow you whole, like when Aunty Betty brought three members of the women's auxiliary home for tea, only to find Uncle Norman splayed out on the couch in his underwear.

I wanted to dash under the table. I could feel my legs moving, but I wasn't going anywhere. This was due to my dad's huge hand on the back of my collar preventing that means of escape. My mother was in her element, my dad was stoic, and my brother was waving courteously to the other guests; wow! Then, when I thought it couldn't get any worse, it did. My parents kissed, and the room cheered. The only utensil within reach by which I could possibly end my life was a melon spoon, which, though clumsy and probably very bloody and painful, would have worked. Sadly, I couldn't reach it.

Eventually, we were seated. I looked at the flowers littering the table and imagined having laser-powered eyes that could eviscerate the flowers with one glance. Then I looked at my preening brother and realised why God had not given me laser-powered eyes with the capacity to obliterate. As if all this was not traumatic enough, I had noticed that my brother was acting strangely. He kept gazing across the room where another family was dining. Suddenly, the gangly creature in the corner waggled her long, bony fingers in our direction. I turned in time to see my brother waving back with a strange smile on his face. It was enough to make you throw up your melon balls. My brother and a girl.

This girl had obviously taken a fancy to him. It would be easy for me to excuse the girl by mentioning that her menu was in brail or that her guide dog was so well behaved but having what seemed like perfect vision she lacked any excuse at all. My brother was fourteen. I heard that strange things happened to you at that age. My friend Wolfy's brother had gone to bed one night and woken up the next morning with a full beard. When he appeared at breakfast and asked where the marmalade was in a deep bass voice, it both alarmed his mother and scared the dog.

At length, my brother asked my dad if he could walk on the beach after dinner. I knew something was up because normally, he would rotate his socks, trim his nose hair, sip his cocoa, and go to bed. He would then listen to the weather reports for the Outer Hebrides and the Icelandic passage before going to sleep. Not tonight, it seemed; he had other plans. This was way too good to miss.

Subtlety was not my brother's strength. When he came back from my parents' room, he reeked of Old Spice, and his hair was plastered down with Brylcreem. He was also beetroot red from sitting in the sun all day, so he looked like a cherry lollipop that had been dipped in chip fat. He put on his hideous blazer and tie and told me to stay in the room under penalty of death, to which I said I absolutely would.

I followed him out of the hotel and to the seafront. The sun was going down, and it might have been a very romantic setting for any other two people. I kept my distance as he headed for the bandstand on the promenade. Sure enough, this was the rendezvous point; there she was. They were both nervous; it took them three attempts to hold hands. She was taller than him and wiry thin, so their attempts to put their arms around each other as they walked down the prom had a painful choreography as they tried to match each other's stride. This, combined with the uneven incline, which naturally increased their pace, made them look like they were coming up fast in the outside lane of a three-legged race. They took off down the prom and sat on a bench in front of some privet bushes.

I had to stand on a rock to look over the hedge. It gave me a perfect vantage point. I watched the awkward posturing as he attempted to kiss her. They both kept moving their heads in a threatening manner, like two Chilean llamas vying for dominance. Finally, he went for it. He missed of course. His gaping and slobbering mouth engulfed her nose completely. It was what I imagined it would be like being attacked by a mutant goldfish! He finally disengaged, and she wiped her nose with a handkerchief. It was just as he was about to give her a second slobbering that I fell off the rock and into the bushes, impaling myself on the privets.

Of course, I was close enough to gain their attention. "What is that?" she cried. "That," he yelled loud enough for me to hear, "is my little and soon-to-be deceased brother." Those were the last words I heard before he set off in my direction. Extricating myself from the hedge, I began running up the road toward the hotel as fast as my pusillanimous little legs would go. It was a desperate attempt to reach the hotel and the possible safety of my parents. It was not to be. In Napoleonic parlance, my escape attempt was a forlorn hope, an attempt from which there is little chance of survival. No matter how fast I ran, it wasn't fast enough, and it was not too long before I smelled the ominous scent of Old Spice very close behind me. Then, in an instant, it was all over. I found myself pinned against a lamppost facing a very red-faced and irate brother, his shiny Brylcreemed head glistening in the lamplight as he prepared to dismember me.

I saw both fists raised as he was about to begin the pummelling of a lifetime. A very short lifetime. Only the arrival of the girl saved me from the dubious joys of sucking hospital food through a straw for the next three months. She urged him to let me go so they could continue their date. At that moment, I realized just how truly beautiful this plain girl from Tunbridge Wells really was; indeed, at that exact moment, she had an inner light that shone out of her like a saint - flooding the world with mercy and kindness. I will be forever grateful to the girl who saved my young life that night.

Later, when he finally arrived back at the hotel, he had calmed down considerably. Apparently, he had finally worked out which part of her face his lips were supposed to engage and so was of a less murderous temperament. It did not stop him from beating me, though, which he did until my dad heard the noise next door and carted him off for a talking-to. When he returned, he was about to resume the beating when I offered him a deal: my life in return for not telling my parents where he had been and what he had been up to, and also by telling his friends what I had seen, embellishing it some by possibly describing the girl as something akin to Raquel Welch and him as some type of suave lothario to his friends. Well, it could be possible in the *Twilight Zone* or some other form of altered consciousness.

It was at this point that he repented of the evil he would visit upon me and agreed. I was seeing life through the eyes of a boy, whose sentence commuted, had a new appreciation of life and of girls, whose beauty I now realised was considerably more than just skin deep, and that grace and kindness make women truly beautiful, not just their looks.

Julie got to hang out with our family that week, and we became good friends. She was a wonderful and caring person who exhibited great confidence and kindness and gave me an entirely different perspective on girls. My brother was gone every evening after dinner for the remaining days of our holiday. The sun continued to shine, and the sandy beaches of Tenby, warmed by its heat, offered endless fun. The sea and sky were very blue that week in June, the kind of blue that only belongs to childhood.

My journal did record one other event that happened that week, and the impact it seemed to have on my dad. The 5th of June 1968, the day of my pummelling and my parent's silver wedding anniversary, was soft and warm with clear blue skies. It was there on the beach that we heard the news of Bobby Kennedy's assassination on our old red radio. I remember watching my dad wander off down the beach alone, lost in his thoughts. Thirty years later, I would drive past the Ambassador Hotel, the site of the shooting on my way to work every day. It was no longer operating as a hotel by then, but it was a constant reminder. There wasn't a day went by passing that hotel when I didn't think of that week in Tenby in the early summer of 1968.

A week later we returned home. Even in Manchester, the west wind blew soft and warm, the grass was green, and the scent of clematis and jasmine hung in the air like a gentle benediction. The cricket House matches, which were always played at the end of June, were soon upon us. That year, we made it to the final. Our match with Brindley would be remembered as the most exciting game in the school's history and was best reflected in the extraordinary achievement of one boy.

Chapter 16

Nick of Time

H ow had it come to this? How had it come to be that it was June, and I had spent every Saturday afternoon since Christmas tending the yard for my dad, tidying my bedroom for my mother, and helping my brother rebuild his two-thousand-piece model replica of the ship, 'Indefatigable,' that had mysteriously been smashed to smithereens the previous year, instead of being out with the lads? Six months of this without any hope of reprieve. Unfortunately, I knew the answer all too well. Money! The love of money really was the root of all evil, hence these chores and all their adjacent misery.

The problem was that all this was my fault, well, except for Big George, who was also to blame, and Cynthia Hardcastle, who might well be a goddess but was also a very fickle goddess. Not to mention Nick Robertson, who, though not actively involved, nevertheless played his part. So, come to think of it, very little if any of this was my fault. I was the victim of bad timing and unfortunate circumstances.

These deductions did nothing to improve my mood. It had all started six months earlier at the school Christmas party, an event which, from that day forward, would no longer elicit in me, feelings of great joy and goodwill to all men. I had it on good authority that something unique was to happen before Father Christmas came into the main hall to give out his gifts. Funded as they were by the Board of

Education, the gifts were extremely paltry. Kids were antic- ipating Scalextric, railway sets, footballs, Subbuteo games, possibly the odd bicycle, and whatever it was that girls liked. All we got was a festive-looking bag containing a paper hat, a kazoo, and a packet of Swizzles, which were aptly named based on the bag's contents.

It was a disturbing coincidence that Father Christmas not only looked like Mr Balinsky, our school caretaker but our unworthy Christmas gifts were also stored in his little clos- et. Last year's party started me thinking as I scrutinised what kind of Father Christmas gave such chintzy gifts. Could Mr Balinsky, our caretaker, really be him? I do not know what Father Christmas wore under his red uniform, but I am pretty sure it was not standard British government Board of Education overalls, under which he sported a heart-shaped tattoo that read, 'Myra loves her handyman.'

This year, the school board wanted to make everything more dramatic. To mask Father Christmas' appearance, the lights would be turned off for a whole minute while he placed himself in the middle of the room, and then they would be turned on with him in place to rousing cheers and applause. I worked out that a full minute in the dark would give me enough time to put my foolproof plan into effect, after which everything would be right with the world forev- er. My informant was none other than Jingo Shuttleworth, whose aunt was best friends with Miss Collingwood, my teacher. Jingo assured me that this information was both secret and trustworthy. I planned to sit opposite Cynthia Hardcastle while the lights were off. Then, in the darkness unseen by anyone, I would let her know how I felt about her. It was brilliant and foolproof.

I had to be careful, though; during the party rehearsal, Miss Collingwood had made us practice barn dances. One of them to the tune of 'The Grand Old Duke of York,' which, if sung to the words we used behind the bike sheds, you would find yourself in the Bat Cave getting a good whacking from our Headmaster, Mugger Murdoch.

This was not the only danger. Ginger Tompkins, who played goalkeeper for our school team, held hands with Gloria Cookson during one of the dances. This was judged to be okay by the lads as everyone was forced to do it during the dancing unless they were thought to be enjoying it, in which case, you were quickly summoned to the boy's room, where a hastily assembled grand jury of your peers heard you out to see if there was enough evidence to proceed to trial. As I had already survived one such ordeal during the Man from U.N.C.L.E. invisible ink ordeal, I was in no hurry to repeat it. Hence, my brilliant plan. I would declare my love to Cynthia under the cloak of darkness; it was nothing short of brilliant!

The night of the Christmas party came with great excitement and anticipation. The moment arrived when the music and the dancing stopped, and we were all asked to sit. It could not have been any more perfect. Cynthia was sitting at a table in the corner opposite Tiny Teddy Fothergill, the smallest boy in the school. Teddy was straining to see her over the top of the table, having both arms raised above his head, frantically feeling around the tabletop, trying to find his half-eaten and elusive pork pie.

I sauntered to Teddy's table just before the lights went out and informed him that his mother had arrived at the front gate with his booster seat. He asked me to guard his chair while he was gone, which I was more than willing to do. I sat down and smiled across the table at a vision of beauty. Cynthia Hardcastle was now opposite me in all her resplendent loveliness. This was too easy; the enormity of my own genius almost overcame me.

The lights went out, and there was a momentary yell from someone at the other end of the room, telling me Wolfy had found Henrietta Pross, Cynthia's best friend. For some extraordinary reason, Wolfy had a crush on Henrietta; he once declared that she only had one flaw, "I know," I responded, "her personality," which was so poisonous that we suspected she had been slain by Perseus in a previous life. I was aware of some commotion during this brief interlude but paid no mind to it and launched into my long-awaited profession of love.

When the lights came on, I prepared to be dazzled by Cynthia's beaming smile, only to find myself waking to a living nightmare: the one where Cynthia Hardcastle turns into Big George. Big George was the biggest boy in school, and there he sat, gazing at me with a bemused look. He pushed an apple pie into his mouth with both hands. "You know, you are supposed to eat that by the slice, George, don't you?" I said as nonchalantly as I could. George mumbled something unintelligible in reply. He made one large swallow, licked his thick lips, gazed at me with expressionless eyes, and then spoke. "I am flattered," he said, "that you think the sun rises and falls at the behest of my smile, and I am very excited that you should want to carry my bag home every day after school," he said flatly. "And," he paused long enough to allow his tongue to reach a large crumb of apple pie that had somehow eluded his huge mouth, 'if it was the right film, I would be delighted to go to the pictures with you, but and I can't state this strongly enough, under no circumstances will there be any kissing," he said emphatically. He then added, "Are you finished with that iced bun?" I gazed over at Cynthia, who was now sitting opposite Nick Robertson and sporting a large grin.

My plan might have been foolproof, but it obviously wasn't original. She had the same idea. Now, it would begin. The piper would have to be paid, and the price would be stiff, to say the least. The price of George's silence would be paid in pork pies, cheese and onion crisps, chocolate biscuits, Curly Wurleys, Walnut Whips, Bar Sixes, Bon Bons, Marathon bars, and iced buns, just like the one that had been on my plate and was now filling his rosy cheeks.

This is why, at nine, my life was over. Feeding Big George demanded much more than my pitiful allowance. Rumour had it that Big George's parents and four sisters all lived in a hole in the ground on the old bomb site at the back of Starkey Street so they could afford to feed him. However, it now became clear that no matter how many years I had left in this world, they would all be spent washing windows, carrying out laundry, moving the prop, and weeding the garden until I was old and dishevelled. Then, I would be sent to be with other worn-out men with no ability, talent, or hope of success, which meant I would end up playing for Sheffield United. It was just all too hard to bear.

It was now June, and for six months, all my spare time was spent earning money to buy George's silence. Ironically enough, Nick Robertson would come to my rescue in a very roundabout way. Nick was eleven and in his last year at school. I might have known that a fickle goddess like Cynthia Hardcastle went for older men. Nick was the Head Prefect at our school. Prefects were the social and intellectual elite, forged from the crucible of common sense and brimming with responsibility. It was their job to monitor the rest of us: the great unwashed that made up most of the school. Usually, we detested the prefects, who were a bunch of geeks overall, but Nick was different. He was nice-looking, stocky, athletic, and, most of all, kind. He was the blond-haired, broad-shouldered hero of the ribboned coat, my House, and the school cricket captain.

Our school had Houses in those days, of which there were four, and every student belonged to one of them. They were usually named after great men of England's past: Edward Elgar, Joshua Reynolds, Robert Falcon Scott, Timothy Dalton, etc. Our school's four Houses were all named after the local landed gentry of the past. Each House competed against the others in sports and academics. They also had four distinct House colours. Ours was yellow, which was mostly an accurate representation of our character, which proved itself best in our House cricket matches that year. It was the House cricket match that eventually squared things for me with Big George.

Wolfy suggested that if Big George put on a white shirt, he could participate as the sight screen, moving from end to end at the close of each over. But George wanted to play, and he told me that we would be even if he got picked for the House cricket eleven. So, I set about getting George selected. Wolfy was our vice-captain and our fast bowler. Wolfy said George would have to prove himself by passing a fitness test if he wanted to play. George did not like the sound of that, and I thought for a moment that he was hyperventilating in his pie wrapper, but to everyone's relief, he was just licking the grease from the bottom of the chip paper. George agreed to show up on Saturday morning and take the fitness test.

Saturday came, and I found myself on the village green with Limpy, Mike, and Wolfy, who was administering the test. George arrived looking like a much less athletic version of Billy Bunter in a white T-shirt and calf-length black shorts.

The first test was a standing jump. Wolfy blew his whistle and shouted," Jump!" George gathered himself, dipped his knees, bent his elbows, and forced himself up with a gargantuan effort before slumping back to his usual posture, out of breath but obviously pleased with himself. "Aren't his feet supposed to leave the ground?" Wolfy said with undisguised sarcasm.

"He was very close," I said.

" Moving on," said Wolfy. The second test was catching. Wolfy produced a cricket ball and tossed it to George. The ball went over George's left shoulder and landed on the grass. "Ready?" said George, looking at Wolfy. I was desperate. I grabbed Mikey's Mars bar from his hand and threw it at George. He plucked the chocolate bar from mid-air with lightening alacrity, had the wrapper off, and it was halfway down his throat before any of us could react. "See that," I shouted at Wolfy; he was less than impressed.

"They are not going to be hitting Mars bars at us," he remarked churlishly. This was not going well at all. One test left for George. It was the hundred-yard dash. George heard the word 'Go' and set off for the finish line a hundred yards away. We walked down to the finish line to wait for him. We talked about the England team, Sir Alf Ramsay, the upcoming test match with India, Captain Pugwash, and Doctor Who's latest episodes. Limpy read a chapter from his new book by Ryder Haggard, which was very exciting. It prompted an argument as to where Africa was, whether it was north or south of London. We drifted off to the local paper shop, where we each bought and drank a Vimto before strolling back to the finish line. A very sweaty George was now only ten yards from the finish line and breathing heavily. An hour later, after George's mother had come and picked him up in their family lorry, Wolfy announced his decision. Wolfy declared that after weighing everything up, George would not make the team.

George did, however, make the team. It was against all the odds, which was good news for me. Nick Robertson had heard what we did in giving George a fitness test and was not best pleased that we had put George through that ordeal. He apologised to George on our behalf and made Wolfy offer him a starting spot on the team. He explained to us afterward that even though George, on merit, did not deserve to play, what we had done was unkind and wrong, and therefore, he said, "George could play."

This was the type of kid Nick was, and it was not an isolated incident either. Bingo Barret's sister Maureen, who was in our class, had leukaemia. We were unsure what that was but knew it wasn't good. Nick knew what it was and that she was fighting for her life. She had a crush on Nick, but then again, which girl did not? He visited her at the hospital and home every Saturday morning that year, even after school was out.

Nick was enormously popular with everyone, especially the kids on our House team. Wolfy and I idolised him, and so did Cynthia. It was the final of the House matches against Brindley House that reflected Nick's character best. That year, he was Captain, and to be honest, he was our only decent player except for Wolfy, our fast bowler. Flitcroft could bat a bit, but that was it. The game had been de-layed due to rain showers, so it started late. We lost the toss, which meant we would bat last and, because of the delay, would have to deal with the fading light. Brindley was batting first and reached 91 in their allotted overs, which does not sound like much, but it was a useful score on that pitch that night. They also had Johnny Todd. Toddy was unusually tall for his age, tall and gangly, the perfect physique for a fast bowler. Nick told us not to be afraid of him and that we should look him in the eye, which was rather difficult without a chair to stand on.

Nick had outthought Toddy when he was at the crease batting, by placing Big George at long mid-off. Toddy knew if he hit the ball out there anywhere near Big George, it would be time for maths class tomorrow morning before George would throw the ball in. Unfortunately for Toddy, he hit it straight to George. George was not mobile, but he did have an arm, and he pinged that ball back like a cannon, hitting the wicket and running Toddy out.

Toddy's prowess, however, was in fast bowling; he was very fast. You did not so much see the ball as smell it as it whizzed beneath your nose or buzzed past your ear or parted your hair. Consequently, there was much fear and trepidation in the ranks as we prepared to bat. This conspicuous lack of moral fibre was best reflected in our House colour, yellow, which was rapidly turning brown the faster Toddy bowled. Our House motto was 'Oh fructus fructus,' which loosely and politely translated from the Latin means, 'Oh dear, that's not good.' Most of our team was in and out quicker than Wolfy's monthly bath.

Nick opened the batting and remained steady throughout. He was a solid bat, and he had guts. The rest of us were steadfastly trying to determine where the ball was going to be and then trying to be somewhere else. Occasionally, we would get it wrong, and the ball would hit us and trickle off for runs. Apart from Nick, who remained calm and scored consistently, most of us got a goose egg on the old scorecard, and we looked rather more relieved than disappointed when Toddy sent our wickets flying into three different postcodes.

Flitcroft was the worst of all of us; with every ball Toddy pinged down, he backed away from the wicket until he eventually found himself taking stance just outside the boy's lavatory in the main hall. There were two minor heroes that evening: Snowy hit a fine quick 20 before Toddy had him caught behind, and the surprise of the evening was Tiny Teddy Fothergill. Nick sawed his bat in half, so it was much lighter, and then he taught him the 'hook shot,' which they practiced all that week. It was usually employed when facing the bouncer, which was a short, fast-pitched delivery that usually ended up around your ears. Still, as every ball was a bouncer to Teddy, he hooked everything. Peering out between his pads and wearing his school cap, he swotted at Toddy's missiles, swiping away above his head and occasionally edging one off to the third-man boundary for four. When they ran between the wickets, it looked like something Pablo Picasso might have painted during his bizarre period, depicting a Greek god and a constipated penguin with a large hammer playing cricket on a summer's eve.

Eventually, Teddy was out for 15. I was batting last, and as anyone who had ever seen me bat will tell you; it was still too far up the batting order. So, I was out there to simply hang around and try to let Nick, who had carried his bat, finish the job.

We needed seven to win the match. It was very late in the evening when I came to the crease. The sun hung low in a quickly darkening sky that flashed gold and crimson as the last heat of the day drained away into the west. A hush had fallen around the field in the warm, lazy twilight as the excitement built toward a rousing climax. At the other end of the wicket stood the stuff of legends. Nick was closing in on his half-century; he had carried his bat and earned us at least the opportunity of victory. I still had to face Toddy. The first three balls came within a whisker of my head; the fourth had an invitation to Manchester Royal Hospital pinned to it.

I survived the over but failed to score. Nick faced Tommy Prendergast, who, though slower than Toddy, was not slow. By now, the light was fading fast; the purple twilight had almost entirely surrendered to the encroaching darkness. Yet, there he stood on a bumping pitch in a blinding light, seven to make and the match to win, a Captain's stand with me the last man in. The first ball from Prendergast to Nick came back viciously, and he managed to keep it down. The second caught him, a real stinger above the pad, but he did not rub his leg. The third one, he glanced to long leg, and we ran two. He strained to see now through the deepening night; the fourth ball caught him on the elbow, but again, he said nothing. The umpires might have stopped play because of bad light if we had not been so close to a result. In those days, it was a case of play up and play the game.

The crowd oohed and aahed at every ball, stroke or miss. The fifth ball he steered through the covers for two, and I ambled back gratefully to the relative safety of the non-striker's end as the crowd cheered. I will never forget the moment before that last ball, as he stood there with his easy grin framed against the purple night. He took a deep breath and came to the crease. Tommy flew in competitive to the end, this was the last ball of the match, and three were still needed to draw and four to win. The ball was of good length and line, and it seemed as if Tommy had won it for Brindley House. The ball landed directly in line with Nick's off-stick. He stepped back and flashed it away through backward point for four runs and the match. We had won the cup! The crowd cheered and invaded the field, chairing Nick off like the champion he was.

The parents were thrilled to see the presentation of the Cricket trophy handed to Edgeworth House and its Captain Fantastic. It was a night that lived long in our memories, and the annuls of House lore: a cheering crowd and a boy with a cup late one summer's evening fifty years ago. In later life, I would think back on that game and realise that even though Toddy took six wickets that night, an incredible feat, it was a batter playing against all the odds, as well as the pitch and the light, that taught me a lesson I would never forget; that there are other things than size, speed, and skill. There is character and courage, two virtues that inspired a team to victory, and at least one boy who would remember these moments for the rest of his life.

I still have my medal from that victory, a little tarnished now, but just as precious as it was then. Maureen Barker fought hard and well in her battle for life. The leukaemia went into remission, and she returned to school the next year. It never returned. She grew up to graduate from Nursing school, married a Scotsman, and had four children. She worked in several Scottish hospitals, always in the children's wards, not unlike the one where she fought for her life when she was young. Perhaps it was as a tribute to the doctors, nurses, and staff who fought with her and for her all those years ago.

She retired not long ago and enjoys spending time with her grandchildren in the untamed wilds of the Scottish Highlands.

Nicholas Colin Robertson died on the 17th of November 1968; he was eleven years old. He was crossing the street close to his home when he was struck by a car. It was nobody's fault. A dark and cold November was made darker yet by his leaving. In the years to come, when I visited his grave, as I did many times, I could never picture him there as an eleven-year-old boy. In my mind, he will always be older and infinitely wiser than me. The admiration we all had for Nick comes out so clearly in the journal entries that year, the literal phrase used in the journal to describe him is "the best of us all." He was a boy who always stood up for the underdog, our Captain, who battled through the twilight to win a cup and, with it, so many hearts. This chapter is for him.

The school year was coming to a close and our minds were consumed with the upcoming summer holidays and forgetting about school, my mother's wasn't. She had her mind on another school year, and another school; a school that threatened to upend my entire life and sentence me to a fate worse than anyone could imagine...private school!

Chapter 17
School Days

———◆○◆———

It was now the end of June, and with the House cricket matches behind us and the cup safely ensconced in the school trophy case sporting the yellow ribbons to prove that we were House champions, it looked like the start of a great summer.

However, having survived the threat of nuclear attack, ear acid poisoning, a thrashing from our Headmaster, a ten-ton locomotive, the sinking of the very dubious raft, next-door cats, vampires in the shed, my mother's driving, not to mention her cooking, a raging inferno, murderous rugby games, aristocratic ghosts, and very hard cricket balls, you would have thought there was nothing left to fear. Not so.

Nobody, least of all me, was prepared for a threat equally devastating as all the above. The dark and ominous spectre of private school had suddenly loomed large and foreboding over my future. Even at nine years old, my parents were grooming me for an educational nightmare of horrendous proportions. They had, for some incomprehensible reason, always wanted at least one of their children to show some scholastic aptitude. Like my mother said, if it was not going to happen naturally, then they were going to damn well make it happen.

After an excruciating and mesmerising ten minutes one Sunday morning watching my brother trying to put the top back on the sauce bottle, it became painfully clear to both my parents that he would not be the one to advance the family's hope for academic brilliance. Consequently, the duty had fallen to me as their last best hope. Yes, they were that desperate.

It was then decided in some dark and lamentable corner of our house that I should be the one to go and sit a pre-test at our local private school. I wanted to attend a regular secondary modern school like every other normal kid, but it seemed I was fated for something far worse. There was to be a preliminary exam to see if I warranted the potential expense of a private education. This was the worst possible news. Not only was I to be sacrificed on the altar of intellectual family hubris, but the examination would take place on a Saturday morning, and Saturday mornings were sacrosanct. Those hallowed hours were set aside for playing football with the lads. Only death, or worse, family weddings, could interfere with those golden hours idly spent upon our village green, whether on frosty mornings or sun-kissed Saturdays when the sun shone bright and warm from a summer sky. Worse still, the lads would find out I was to be scrubbed and tubbed, strategically dressed, and shunted off to sit in a hall full of fops and whimsies, with lurid-looking Housemasters warming their crumpets by the fire. My journal records two words at the end of this entry: No Way!

Private school was the type of place where, if you were not careful, a good lad might accidentally trip and get impaled on somebody's stiff upper lip. I knew this because, upon hearing of my potential private school incarceration, my brother had forced me to watch the movie *Tom Brown's*

School Days, where a young and innocent boy is sent to private school and tortured by older, more violent, and feckless youths, who not only toast crumpets by the fire but Tom himself. My brother informed me that roasting young boys was common at private schools and actively encouraged by the masters. He said that there were no sports there either because they had too many fat, wheezy boys with notes from Matron excusing them from all games and that, as a consequence, extra Latin verbs and maths were taught instead, especially to 'stinkers.' Apparently, 'stinkers,' according to my brother - whose knowledge of public school had stemmed from watching the film *Goodbye Mr Chips* more times than is healthy for a boy his age - were what they called new boys. We had a 'stinker' at our school, but he was not a new boy. Nigel 'Pongo' Pittman had been known to clear a room in seconds.

Once, after a school lunch of bubble and squeak and stewed prunes and custard, of which he was allowed two helpings, he cleared the entire main hall. Fortunately for all present, the long and ominous growl that preceded this vile and pernicious act of biological warfare gave warning to the unspeakable horror about to be unleashed. It was terrifying to see Pongo half raising himself from his seat to rest his considerable bulk on both elbows so as not to cause himself bodily injury upon delivery. He then emitted a sound later described by survivors who could still speak as the sound of a huge Viking horn being blown through a series of hollow caves before finally finding its unnatural exit through a gurgling mud pit. In the aftermath of this unholy and terrifying emission, the whole hall fell silent, the air started to move in warm, hazy waves across the room, and everyone there was suddenly overcome by a deep and profound instinct for self-preservation. Panic ensued as a whole room full of innocent women and children instantly headed for the door whilst trying vainly to hold their breath.

Everybody made it out except poor Mrs Pikestaff, our dinner lady, a slight and sensitive woman who was overcome by the first waves before she could reach the door. Once outside, it was not much better; boys and girls with blue faces wept and cried for their mothers whilst others were helped away to receive counselling. After that incident, Pongo was forced to eat his lunch at a specially prepared table in the centre circle of our school football pitch for the rest of that term.

Private school did indeed sound dreadful. This did nothing to alleviate my sense of foreboding. I knew that the sinister force driving this idea was currently in the kitchen making fruitcake. There was only one force in the universe, except for God Himself, who could make it change its mind, and he was in our garden shed trying to fix the vacuum cleaner.

It was Saturday, and my dad liked to retreat to the garden shed in the afternoon to recover from the shopping trip my mother subjected him to every Saturday morning. Uncle Norman had arrived an hour earlier, and I think they had been visited by Mr Walker, or good old Johnnie as Uncle Norman called him. They were listening to the test match on the radio; England were playing India and doing rather well. Somebody called Boycott had been batting for three weeks and only scored four runs; my father and Uncle Norman thought this was grand stuff from an English opening bat. Uncle Norman said Boycott was not a bad chap, really, even though he was born in Yorkshire. Uncle Norman said it was a shame anyone had to be born in Yorkshire, and that the government should take measures to protect people from that happening to them.

They were both in an exceptionally good mood; Mr Walker must have stayed a while because there was much mutual mirth and congratulation. There were other clues as to their possible inebriation, such as Uncle Norman having no luck getting better radio reception no matter how carefully he moved the dials on my mother's sewing machine. This, combined with the fact that my dad, who was attempting to fix the Hoover, had twice tried to plug it into the rabbit hutch, led me to believe that Mr Walker's presence was still being felt. Neither the vacuum cleaner nor the rabbit hutch were whirring into life no matter how many times my dad tried, which drew a frown from my mother when she suddenly appeared like an apparition in the room. This made both my dad and Uncle Norman sit up straight, immediately subduing the mirth and frivolity. Brian Johnston, the commentator on the radio, was talking about Pocock and Titmus, which prompted my mother to inquire of my father whether this was suitable listening material for a future private school boy. He replied that they were both English spin bowlers, to which she replied, "See that they are," and left.

This was the perfect moment to raise the issue at hand. Uncle Norman and Frosty the Rabbit were both sacked out, and my dad was trying to focus on the fan belt on the Hoover. I laid out my concerns as best I could, to which he replied,

"There are some forces in this world it's best not to mess with, son."

"Girls?" I proffered.

"Precisely," he responded. "It's best not to mess with them until you are older and much stronger," he continued.

"Girls are confusing," I said. They don't think like us."

"You learn fast," he replied. On the one hand, there was Cynthia Hardcastle, who truly was a goddess, a girl that could make you give up your lunch, and then there was Paula Postlethwaite, a squib of a girl who lived in the house behind ours. She, too, could make you give up your lunch, but in a much less pleasant way.

It was true, though, that girls did wield awesome power. My mother could delight my dad or drive him to the shed with equal alacrity. He was my last great hope. When all was said and done, and as much as he loved to please her, when he made the final decision, that was it; it was a tenuous thread for the rest of your life to hang by. "You could make her not send me." There it was, I had said it. He thought for a moment like a man mentally flipping through the future chapters of a very long book and intently noting how things might unfold for him if he were to make a false step.

At last, he said, "You couldn't possibly live long enough or work hard enough to repay me for that one," he said knowingly. He was not unsympathetic to my cause, though. "Look," he said, "I will see what I can do." That was the best I could hope for. My only hope lay in the fact that I knew he did not want two fops in the family and that, like Geppetto, he wanted at least one real boy.

I could always run away I thought, as I meandered back to the house. I could go south, but then that would be the same as going to private school, even worse because you would have to live there. There was always Liverpool, where, according to Billingsley, they didn't even have schools. I knew no one would ever come looking for me there, but that was perhaps too extreme. Wales was a possibility, but again, according to Billingsley, kids there didn't leave school until they were twenty-four. Fifteen more years of school was unthinkable. Or Scotland, but then there would be haggis and dubious health services. According to Beaky, his Grandad had been playing golf in the highlands as a young man when he sprained his ankle. In those days in the Scottish Highlands, there were very few doctors; in fact, anyone who had watched every episode of Dr Finlay's Casebook qualified as a doctor. Beaky said that his Grandad was examined by an old doctor who had graduated from the Glenfiddich School of Anaesthesiology in 1901 and whose office motto, according to the plaque on the wall, was 'if in doubt, cut it off. 'I didn't want anything cutting off, so that was out of the question.

It was no good. I would have to unpack my small bag with my action man, my 1967 *Topical Times* with a full colour photo of Andy Lochhead, (which I still have), my three *Beano* annuals, a half-eaten Marathon bar, six of my favourite marbles, and Eddie, my pet beetle who I had found in the garden shed. Eddie was even now living in fear for his life after being tried and convicted in absentia by that same military Junta that wanted to send me to public school. Eddie would have been happy to go to Liverpool, as beetles seemed very popular there. No, it would take a miracle to get out of this.

Even my dad had failed on this one. My mother's will was irrevocable; the die seemed all but cast when, low and behold, a high-speed incident changed everything.

My Uncle David arrived a few days before I was due to sit the dreaded public school suitability test. Everyone loved Uncle David, for he was a good man, despite living on the Isle of Man, where, according to Billingsley, three-legged men chased cats with no tails around glens filled with fairies. Uncle David said it was a sedate place. Apparently, someone had declared a bank holiday there in 1933 and forgot to tell anyone it was over. He had been a teacher and Headmaster all his life, so I always stood on the other side of his cane hand.

My mother was overjoyed that he had suddenly appeared. She revered him and his achievements, as he was the golden boy of the family, so much so that my middle name was in honour of him. I loved him because he was smart, cool, and funny, and he loved football. He would talk to me about Bobby Tambling's goal record at Chelsea, Bobby Moore's imperious playing style, and whether I thought Bolton would ever win another game during my lifetime, and, as I was already nine years old, I doubted it.

David Eccles was the spin bowler on our school cricket team. He was a star in his own galaxy. He was skilled, determined, tenacious, and fearless. Girls swooned when he appeared; even Cynthia Hardcastle's pulse had been known to beat faster at his smile. He was a legend. It was his bravery that ultimately was to reshape future events.

Every Thursday evening toward the end of the school year, we had box cart races down the big hill just outside our school. It was safe because it was in the back of a housing division with very little traffic, and we usually blocked the only adjoining road. We were the first of the *Fast and the Furious*, and David Eccles was the Vin Diesel of our primary school, except he had hair. Wolfy drove our cart. He was highly qualified, too, passing all the required tests to race a wooden cart with homemade wheels downhill at break-neck speed with no brakes. His chief qualification being that there was absolutely no history of sanity whatsoever in his family. Beaky had built the "Intrepid" and had assured us that it was safe, just like the raft he built when we crossed old farmer Newton's big pond. The raft sank with all hands on the frantic return journey!

That night, David Eccles and his crew introduced the Silver Bullet to the world. It was a lightweight box construction, with an angled-down chassis attached to a set of huge pram wheels. This was cutting-edge, innovative stuff. It looked awesome and dangerous. Eccles and his crew had tested it out, and it was fast, but not suicidally fast, as the wheels were sufficiently rusty enough to help as a natural brake. They were about to break all kinds of records. At the bottom of the hill was the finish line. There was a little straightaway to slow you down, then the safety zone, a strip of soft grass about fifteen yards long, for emergency evacuations. There had been many sudden evacuations on this hill over the years, some of them without ever leaving the cart.

Beyond the grass were two entrances: to the left was the school gate, which took you into the front playground, and to the right was the entrance to the local orphanage.

Who would have thought that I would owe not going to public school to Soapy Saunders's dad? The Eccles crew had left the four-wheeler at Soapy's house while they were at school because it was closer to the hill. Soapy's dad, in a bid to help, noticed the rust on the wheels and sprayed them with WD40. The rest of the events of that epic evening belong to history. At precisely 5:41 pm on Thursday, October 5th, strapped to the front of the Bullet, David Eccles flew into history, shattering every record ever set on the hill. He flashed down the incline at a frightening speed and literally screamed through the finish line. He then veered right at an unbelievable speed, blazing over the grass and disappearing into the orphanage, approaching something close to Mach One.

Nothing more was heard from him or about him until the next afternoon. Rumours swirled and abounded that night and the next morning when he did not show up for school. Some said he was dead, others that he had achieved flight, and some that he had crashed through the front doors of the orphanage and had been adopted by a visiting family from Romania and was even now on route to Bucharest by way of a traveller's caravan.

It was, however, revealed on Friday afternoon that he was both alive and well and still in England. In fact, he was at home with a twisted ankle and a sprained wrist, which was a relief to us all. Later that afternoon, I was summoned to Mr. Johnson's room at school. Mr Johnson was the deputy Headmaster and the school cricket coach. M Johnson informed me that due to David's injuries, he would not be playing for the school team and that I was selected as his replacement for the next day's game. This was the moment I had been waiting for, the pinnacle of my young life. This was better than chips, gluing the lid on my brother's Tupperware lunch container, and even kissing Cynthia Hardcastle. Well, maybe not that good. I was to represent my school against Hulton Street West, our archenemy, but wait I had that infernal exam.

That thought was all it took to bring my world crashing down around my feet. What was I to do, had I reached the zenith of my dreams only to have them dashed on the rock pile of private education? I could turn to drink, but not even Vimto could drown these sorrows. I thought of the words of that great twentieth-century philosopher Julie Andrews, but even the thought of a few whisker-less kittens hanging on your nose and eyelashes, all covered in strudel and tied up with string, did not help. Even the thought of when Eddie had crawled down my brother's shirt and the bizarre, almost Caribbean-like festive dance it elicited, as he contorted and gyrated while emitting high and unnatural screams in what sounded very much like the Swahili dialect, could not lighten my mood. Well, not enough to lift the fog of despair that had descended upon me. It was all too much.

I walked home, dragging my satchel behind me. Eventually, I arrived home, entered the kitchen, and told my dad and Uncle David what had happened. "Your mother is set on you taking that test, you know," my dad said.

"I know," I said sadly.

"Go tell her your news; maybe she will relent," said Uncle David kindly. I knew my mother had her heart set on me going to private school, and even then, at that age, I knew she would let me play but be disappointed, and that was worse than taking the test. I told my dad and Uncle David that I would not tell her and would take the test the next morning.

I now had to go and call Mr. Johnson and tell him I could not play. As I came into the hall to use the phone, my mother was just hanging up. Extraordinary, she said loudly, quite extraordinary. That was the school, she said with an air of incredulity; the exam had been postponed. Apparently, the pipes in the main hall had burst, and they were unable to fix them, consequently, there was flooding in the school, and they had to send all the pupils home. No exam, I repeated to myself; "Oh, that's too bad," my dad and Uncle David said almost in unrehearsed unison and with only the slightest air of authenticity. My mother shook her head and walked off to the kitchen. The only person who was not happy was my brother, who claimed he was being ignored despite holding his unopened Tupperware lunch container in his hand and pointing at me wild-eyed and yelling: "He did it; he glued it shut!" But no one really cared. The game the next day was close, but like my brush with private education, we just about edged it, winning by 14 runs.

It had been a close call; disaster had been averted at the last minute by some unknown caretaker's neglected waterworks. However, no sooner had I successfully navigated one crisis than there was another. The whole Bolton Wanderers football team had suddenly vanished from the face of the Earth.

July

Chapter 18
The Crisis

I t was amazing how much Bolton Wanderers factored in the journal, a definite sign of how much my mental faculties had not yet fully developed. Finally, it was July, and only one week was left before the big school holiday. The weather was glorious, and the whole school was ready to be done. However, there was a crisis just as we were all winding down and looking forward to six weeks of freedom. This was a crisis! A real bona fide, grade-A crisis. The entire Bolton Wanderers soccer team had gone missing. I know, Bolton fans said that every Saturday as they trudged disconsolately home from Burnden Park, but this was truly a disaster.

Of course, this was not the real Bolton Wanderers; nobody could get that lucky, but my Subbuteo team, Bolton Wanderers. Subbuteo Bolton was not where they were supposed to be, which was in their box. Subbuteo was a table soccer game complete with a green baize cloth pitch, a set of two goals, a ball, and as many teams as you wanted to buy, which included eleven players and a sub in case the dog ate one.

Bolton was my favourite team; each player decked out with a white shirt, black shorts, and white socks, each painstakingly numbered in red paint by my fair hand, so I knew who each of them was when I commented on the games. The numbers were important as all the players looked the same, which, according to Uncle Norman, was just like those hill folk from the back end of Yorkshire who come down to shop together every Thursday afternoon. I had set it all up in my bedroom, and most of the time, I played against my friends or myself; when this happened, I tried to be impartial, but Liverpool kept losing 13 – 0.

To make matters worse, the cat had chewed up Emlyn Hughes, and Tommy Smith had no head. But what about my missing Bolton team? The dog might have eaten one or two Bolton players, but not all of them. No, there was only one dog in the house that could make them all disappear simultaneously, and he only had two legs. That's not to say there weren't similarities, though, between my brother and Hondo in both looks and manners.

Of course, I knew full well why he had done it: revenge! Pure, unfiltered hatred. He had for some weeks now been harbouring unpleasant thoughts. It was nothing more than retribution for what had become known in our household as the 'incident' that had occurred during a day out with my dad.

It had been the weekend that my mother and the ladies from the tearoom of our local cricket club had gone to London for their annual 'meeting'. These outings had gone down in local folklore as something akin to the revelry experienced on the Aventine on Friday nights in ancient Rome during the reign of Emperor Nero. Describing all the ladies as her 'big party,' my mother's words almost sounded strangely prophetic. They had travelled to London that weekend by way of Middlesborough after the driver mistakenly asked my mother to help him with the directions. Apparently, the one-hundred-and-forty-mile detour north was not completely in vain, said the hotel valet when they finally arrived in London as he watched the driver unload thirteen empty crates of Newcastle brown ale.

My dad had decided to take us out for the day while my mother was gone for the weekend. I had never known my father to lie, so imagine how shocked I was when he said we were going somewhere nice and ended up in Colwyn Bay. My dad and I got the footy out and kicked around while my brother went off to sail his model yacht; his was such an exciting life. It was lunchtime when the 'incident' occurred. We were sat safely ensconced on the prom, eating chicken leek pies my dad had bought for lunch from a Welsh vendor, who made him pay extra just for being English.

While he was gone getting lunch, my brother had been singing Cliff Richard songs on the bandstand for twenty minutes to a bunch of old folks who were feeble and decrepit and, therefore, unable to save themselves. Consequently, the air was foul with resentment and the smell of mothballs and denture cream. They didn't like it very much at all. There were definitely sinister stirrings amongst the aged pensioners, some of whom had tried to end it all by empaling themselves on their own deckchairs.

The mood was beginning to turn very ugly, with the definite threat of bodily harm. Walking sticks were being raised in anger. Fortunately, my father arrived with the pies. It was then that the idea formed in my mind. His singing, which any court in the land would consider elder abuse, deserved some kind of retribution; after all, what about that poor old woman in the front row who couldn't stand it any longer and had finally passed out during his third rendition of Summer Holiday.

I first spotted them while waiting for my dad to return with the pies. A particularly malevolent and desperate-looking flock of seagulls scavenging further along the prom. They had already dive-bombed some of the elderly folk during their lunch, attempting to snatch their bowls of apple sauce and jelly. One old lady had carelessly left her teeth on the table while she gummed a custard tart to death, only to see a large white malevolent bird swoop down and take off with them.

My brother was very competitive; it had been his undoing on more than one occasion, like the time I had told him that being the only athletic one in the family, I had jumped a particularly high and slatted fence. In reality, I would never dream of attempting to scale it unless I was on a good horse, and even then, I would think twice, as would the horse. Just looking at the fence brought tears to my eyes. Of course, he could not let this go and attempted to clear it and thus prove his superior athleticism. The look on his face when he realised he would not make it is etched forever in my memory. Even now, when the subject is raised in his presence, his beer hand trembles, and a tear bursts from his left eye, and on very cold days, he still walks with a hitch. It was awful; no human being should ever have to utter or hear such a noise as came from his ill-judged and ill-timed leap; stray dogs came from miles around upon hearing that unearthly call.

"I bet you can't hit that buoy with a pebble," I said tauntingly.

"What, the one with the ice cream next to his mother?" he replied.

"Buoy, not boy," I replied testily. "The one in the ocean," I clarified.

"Easy he scoffed, can't be more than forty yards out", he stated confidently.

"You can't throw forty yards," I sneered, "Paula Postleth-waite can throw better than you." That did it. He leaped up. "Watch this frog head," he replied lamely.

"Leave your pie; I'll watch it," I said innocently as I could.

"Not likely," he responded, remembering the maggot incident from our last fishing trip.

Yes, the gratification was most pleasing as I watched him stride off in the sunshine down to the beach. He picked his way across the pebbly shore to the ocean about sixty yards away, pie in hand, it wouldn't be long now. It began with a long, low, blood-curdling shriek from a single scout circling above my brother as he searched for the right pebble to toss. The cry did not go unheeded, or the pie in his hand go unnoticed as the rest of the flock down the prom took off in his general direction. All I remember now is the beating of many wings, the sky becoming shadowy, and an ominous moment of quiet serenity before they descended on mass.

It was the worst mugging I have ever seen! It was truly horrible! The birds landed upon him on mass. From a distance, my brother took on the guise of a fat woman in a feather coat doing a festive Caribbean dance. His shrill, panicked cries drew my father's attention, 'What's he doing?" my father enquired.

"Oh, he's just having fun; you know how much he likes animals," I replied in a jocular tone. By now, there was very little of him visible, which was usually a plus; he was both spinning around and trying to shake himself free; letting go of the pie would have been the obvious solution to any normal, sane person, but not to him. He would go down, pie in hand, which he then did. It was only after the birds and boy all went down together, and he was face down in the pebbles with twelve huge angry seagulls perched on his back, that my dad suspected he was not enjoying himself and ran over to shew the hungry beasts off his less fortunate, less handsome, and let's face it, less intelligent son.

I arrived a few seconds after my dad, as I had to wind the film onto the Kodak camera while I was running. My dad cleared the area, grabbed my brother, and hauled him to his feet. There was a wide-eyed, wild, crazed look about him; it was a pathetic sight. I almost felt sorry for him standing there, almost catatonic, with a white splodge on his shoulder where his assailants, having finished violating him, had left their mark of victory, a stain of disdain to add insult to injury. In his tiny pathetic hand was the vestige of a pie crust, the small but meaningful emblem of a pyrrhic victory.

Somewhere on the sideboard in my office, there is a silver-framed black-and-white picture of those moments after the ordeal that gives the incident a certain timeliness that can be enjoyed over and over again by successive generations. It stands proudly next to a black framed photo of a Morris Minor adorned with garden utensils and bicycle handlebars parked in a bed of chrysanthemums at the bottom of our garden. So, it was because of the 'incident' as it became known that the whole Bolton Wanderers team went missing in the early summer of 1968.

In later years, the whole story would come to light of how my brother had sat in our lounge one slate grey afternoon while I was in school. He had built a primitive catapult by placing a ruler over his favourite pencil sharpener. He then placed each player on the end of the ruler and banged his fist down on the other end. Thus, the entire starting line-up and one substitute were hurtled into the fire.

Apparently, John Byrom had ricocheted off the coal scuttle before flying into the flames, while Gordon Taylor and Warwick Rimmer had gone in together. It was very sad. Losing my team sent me into a dramatic downward spiral. The world had grown a little less lovely, and so feeling all forlorn and unloved, I pushed my Sunday trifle away untouched and waited for adolescence to sweep me away. My mother saved the day and annoyed my brother, who, because of lack of evidence, had gotten away with it and smugly declared that perhaps the entire Bolton team was hiding, overcome by great remorse and shame after realising how much pain they had inflicted upon their long-suffering fans for so long. It was this last comment that spurred my mother into action.

Every year in the spring, our school had its sports day, which was great because we got out of arithmetic and joined up writing and art, which was the worst subject of all of them. I once spent three weeks on a painting I did in class. My teacher, Ms. Forsythe, asked to see it, so I handed it to her. I knew something was amok when she continued to turn it around in her hands while emitting a low humming sound. This continued for several minutes before she asked if I was feeling well.

"It's a very good picture of your friend Wolfy," she said encouragingly.

"It's my dog Hondo," I replied indignantly.

"You must miss him a great deal," she said sympathetically.

"He's still alive," I said even more indignantly.

"Oh dear," she said abjectly. I do hope you are good in other subjects." She then walked off.

Sports day came, and as usual, there was lots of running, jumping, pushing, and shoving, just like the audience making for the exit at our school plays when it was announced that my brother's high school band would be playing through the intermission.

Big George had joined up with Jumbo Butterworth. They had already won the Tug-of-War, beating all comers, including a team in the final, which consisted of Mr. Johnson's junior class, four dinner ladies, nineteen parents, the cricket eleven, and old man Hopkins traction engine. It was very impressive to say the least. Cynthia Hardcastle had won the one-, two- and three-hundred-yard dash along with four other events because she was way faster than any of the other girls in school, and no boy wanted to compete against her. The shock of the day was Prunella Watkins winning the sack race. She was a rather rotund girl and not very athletic. She had about as much chance of winning the race as Bolton Wanderers had of winning the European Cup. Not only did she win it, but she also set a new school record for this event and the long jump. The surprise result might have something to do with whatever it was that Wolfy threw into her sack just as the race pistol went off.

When I returned home, my mother declared that she had found the team, much to my delight and my brother's annoyed perplexity. Having examined the team in their much newer box, I asked where the numbers were, to which my mother replied that the players had somehow gotten into the wash and the numbers had come off. My brother asked if it was an attempt at mass drowning, to which my mother's withering gaze communicated something of very thin ice; he then fell silent and went back to his magazine for collectors of Medieval socks. She then emphasised very strongly that should anything happen to them again, no one would be given the benefit of the doubt, after which my brother slunk away to his room.

It all sounded very strange, but there they were. That was how my mother came to save the entire Bolton Wanderers team and restore a boy's faith not only in his mother but in the equity of things, especially as I had just begun watching the real thing by attending games at Burnden Park, where it became abundantly clear that Bolton did not win anywhere near as often as they did in my bedroom.

July that year was warm, and the end of the school year loomed in our thoughts; academic matters seemed to dissolve in anticipation of the summer holidays. However, just a few days before our last day, strange and weird things were happening on our avenue, due mainly to the strange and weird people who lived there.

Chapter 19
Wolfy's Revenge

It was one of those glorious July days, made all the more lovely by the knowledge that in a couple of days, school would end for another year. We all stood in the middle of the street, gazing at the new anomaly on our avenue. "What is it?" Wolfy asked.

"String," Limpy replied, feeling pleased with himself.

"Yeah, but why is it there?" asked Mikey, articulating all our thoughts.

"Maybe it's a washing line," Ginger replied, his face contorting strangely from too much thinking.

"Who has arms that long?" Snowy said, looking up at the piece of twine.

"Yetis do," replied Beaky informatively. The possibility of a family of Yetis living in Grimley's basement and hanging their washing out on a 100-foot piece of string stretching tautly between Grimley's and Nugent's upstairs windows seemed far-fetched, even for our overactive imaginations.

"What do they wear that needs washing?" asked Snowy.

"Yetis don't have clothes," Beaky informed us.

"Well, what do they do on Sundays for church then?" said Limpy, "Do they go naked?" "They don't go to church; they live in the prophylactics," said Billingsley authoritatively. "It's a mountain range," he went on, "in a country ruled by a llama."

"What's a llama? I mean what do they look like?" asked Wolfy.

"Have you ever seen President De Gaulle?" Beaky asked, "You know that guy that owns France."

"Oh, yeah," he and Topsy said in unison. After all, he was on the news nearly every night, not that we watched it, but our dads did, so we kind of learned by osmosis.

"Well, they look like him," Beaky continued.

" My parents went to France on holiday last year," interjected Ginger, unwrapping an Aztec bar, "and I had to go live with my Auntie Gertie for a week. All we ate was porridge and biscuits."

"Why didn't they take you?" Asked Mike.

"They said it wasn't safe and that small boys were in danger of falling down the holes in their public toilets, never to be seen again," said Ginger sadly.

"What kind of biscuits?" asked Big George, but he was rudely interrupted when Lionel Grimley appeared.

"What are you monkeys doing here?" he said with the superiority of a fifteen-year-old private school-educated oik. "Clear off back to the zoo." Grimley lived next door to me, on the other side of old man Fanshaw and the feral cats. Grimley was a colossal nerd. He and his friend Nugent were always up to something dull, and it was a surprise to all of us that they hadn't already bored themselves to death. He had a narrow oval head with tufts of hair sticking in all directions, slanty eyes, a small mouth above a weak chin, and a pencil neck.

"We can be here if we like pinhead," Wolfy replied. Nugent then appeared from behind him, gesticulating wildly.

"Off with you, you b-b-b-b." He had a bad stammer, and we thought we were all about to have our parentage questioned when he finally spit out "blighters." We looked at Beaky, whose razor-sharp retorts and caustic replies were legendary.

"Blighters, schmighters," he replied.

"Good one, Beaks," we all murmured approvingly.

Nugent was short but wide. He had a mop of long, dank brown hair and a broad face with small eyes and no neck, just shoulders protruding from his ears. "What's that?" asked Limpy, still gazing up and pointing to the taut string passing across the road connecting the upstairs windows of the two houses. Grimley looked at Wolfy in a strange sideways manner that spoke of lofty indifference and utter contempt.

"You," he said, speaking to Wolfy and completely ignoring Limpy.

"Did your mother have any human offspring?" That was the last straw.

"Listen, pinhead," I said, "Are you going to tell us or what?"

"No," said Nugent, but it took him a minute to get it out.

He was getting excited now, "Off with you, you oily ticks, and don't come back," he yelled in his clipped private schoolboy accent. We had a low opinion of private school boys with their hoity-toity attitude. We hated toff school kids more than anything, except possibly Marchbanks' crew. When thinking of Grimley and Nugent, that word my brother called me when my parents weren't within earshot came to mind. Except when he didn't know my mother was cleaning the windows outside and she heard him. She pounced on him with all the speed and ferocity of a honey badger when its young are threatened. It was over in moments and just as grizzly. He was dragged off by the ear to the bathroom where multiple doses of Palmolive were administered to the offending tongue. Despite the severe beatings I received, I could not resist singing, "I'm forever blowing bubbles," every time I saw him after that.

Beaky asked his dad what the string meant because my dad had no clue. Mr. Beaky said it was a means of communication whereby if you punched a hole in the bottom of two open cans, then thread the ends in, and knot them, and the string is taut, you can talk to each other, it is something like a primitive telephone. Mr. Beaky told us he and his friend had done it once with disastrous results. Mr. Beaky and his friend had lived opposite each other, with a busy main road in between. They had stretched their string across the busy road; however, it needed to be higher, and they had failed to plan for the number forty-two bus. The moment the double-decker bus hit the string, both cans went flying down the street indiscriminately, bouncing off parked cars and pedestrians' heads.

We asked Mr. Beaky if the string wasn't taut would it still work. He said no, at which we all murmured our approval. The plan was set, and it was a good one. We would find three or four pairs of old shoes, tie them together, and sling them over the string. That should teach those preening fops not to mess with us.

So, we snuck out into the street and threw them up one pair at a time. Some caught and entwined themselves the first time, and others missed the mark and fell indiscriminately, causing all kinds of mayhem. In the end, we got them all up there until the string sagged under the weight of the shoes. We were in my garage celebrating when a pair of shoddy shoes came flying through the open door, hitting Wolfy squarely on the head. Nugent and Grimley appeared. "Get those things down, you morons," Nugent scrambled out.

"Or what?" said Wolfy, rubbing his head. Wolfy had a strange look in his good eye. I had seen it before, and it didn't bode well.

Wolfy rarely got mad, but he did get even. This was well noted by those who knew the tale of Spotty Chumsworth, a rather scrofulous youth who enjoyed homework and had an unhealthy preoccupation with oversized teddy bears. He was called 'Spotty' due to his rather punctuated complexion. It happened one warm, sunny, sleepy afternoon during joined-up writing class. Wolfy had drunk a whole can of fizzy Vimto at lunch, and the bubbles were stirring. Wolfy had an extraordinary gift: his belch was almost quadrophonic at times. It was impressive. On one occasion, after drinking a whole bottle of Dandelion and Burdock without stopping, he burped an entire rendition of 'God Save the Queen.' On these occasions, the volume was formidable and could be deafening if you were taken unawares. Unable to contain the bubbles, Wolfy had decided to share his talent with the class and, in so doing, outdid himself in scope and volume. The whole class jumped out of their seats: the two girls sitting directly in front of him began to cry, the empty milk bottles rattled in their crates, and the class parrot fell off his perch.

Miss Collingwood, our teacher, was a former librarian who was of a rather delicate and nervous disposition, owing to (as rumour had it) getting on the wrong bus one night while away at a Scrabble tournament. Subsequently, she disappeared into the Welsh hinterland with 43 members of the Merthyr Tydfil male voice choir, who sang 'Men of Harlech' at her for nearly five hours. Eventually, with the aid of copious amounts of narcotics and sundry other medication, she recovered sufficiently to take a job teaching. Having steadied herself after Wolfy's blast, she grabbed her handbag and left the room.

From our classroom window, we could see copious amounts of smoke coming from the staff bathroom window. Ten minutes later, when she was much calmer and more relaxed and carefree than we had ever seen her, she absently inquired what that noise was as she rummaged around for some snack food to eat from her desk drawer. When it became clear a wild animal was not involved, and it was one of her students, the investigation began. Wolfy remained quiet and gazed up with admirable nonchalance. It appeared, at length, that he was going to get away with it when Spotty struck and grassed Wolfy up to the utter infamy of his name and pimply countenance. Wolfy was sent to the Headmaster, and Mugger meted out the appropriate disciplinary measures, resulting in Wolfy carrying an inflatable ring around for the next couple of days. Wolfy did not ask who, or what, or when, or why; he just bided his time and waited for the appropriate moment to get even.

Not long after, an incident occurred in the cafeteria, where upon opening his neatly sealed Tupperware lunch box with sparkly stickers on it, Spotty Chumsworth came face to face with a very irate toad which hopped out from under his crab spread sandwiches and onto the table, causing uproar and mayhem as Spotty and the rest of the girls screamed and ran out into the playground. After that, we called him 'Toadie' until he eventually moved away to Huddersfield, where we believe he went to a special school for future government employees, where he was taught to gaze out of the window all day and ignore telephone calls.

Grimley had sown the wind with Wolfy and might at some point reap the whirlwind. "Get them down," screamed Nugent. "Make us," I said defiantly, knowing my mother was in the kitchen and anyone daring to mess with her cub would reap her terrible wrath, not to mention her rolling pin, which she yielded with expert precision. My dad could attest to this personally after he came home a little worse for wear after Christmas drinks at the office, which induced temporary amnesia, and he forgot the Christmas grocery trip that was supposed to be that afternoon.

Grimley leered. "Well," he said, "if you don't, you will be sorry." Pointy head or not, Grimley was not to be underestimated. He lowered his voice menacingly.

"I am connected," he said.

"You are demented," said Beaky, feeling quietly pleased with himself. Grimley ignored him. "My cousin's best friend's neighbour knows Mad Frankie Foster," he stated emphatically, "and if I ask him, he will come down here with his gang, and that will be the end of all you waste of spaces." I wasn't sure about his grammar, but his threat was sure enough. We had all heard of Mad Frankie Foster, the notorious gangster from Manchester's East End. Frankie was said to have been a nice lad once upon a time, with a kindly disposition, until he went to Birmingham looking for employment and was offered a bank job, which he was delighted to accept. By the time his new employers had blown their way into the vault and cleaned out the deposit boxes, Frankie realised that he probably wasn't going to be a financial adviser. He came back to Manchester several months later, a fully-fledged Crime Lord.

"You have one hour," said Grimley, retreating from the garage.

"He's bluffing," said Snowy.

"Yeah, bluffing," Frothy added. A few others said the same, and we all murmured in agreement. There was a moment of deep silence, and I said, "I'll get the ladder."

"Yeah, better," everyone said all at once. So, we fetched my dad's twenty-foot ladder. My street was a cul-de-sac, so there wasn't a problem with traffic. The problem was that there was nothing to lean the ladder against, so all nine of us would have to hold it while one of us climbed up it and unravelled the shoes. The question was, who was stupid enough to climb to the top of a twenty-foot ladder secured only by ten nine-year-old boys? We all looked at Wolfy.

It never occurred to us to have Nugent release one end of the string so we could pick the footwear up off the ground, and both Nugent and Grimley were having way too much fun to enlighten us. It was precarious, to say the least; everyone was yelling at each other as Wolfy made his way up the ladder. Every time he moved, we had to correct the weight and balance on the ladder, which meant we had to move and rotate with his movements. It looked like a very badly choreographed circus act as the ladder swayed back and forth with Wolfy on top. We were forced to move like a giant spider 'to and fro', from one side of the street to the other. Grimley and Nugent sat there with Nugent's new girlfriend, Paula Postlethwaite, who lived in the house directly behind mine. It appeared Paula was moving up in the world, having dumped Marchbanks after the rugby fiasco, and was now taking up with the older and even more feckless Grimley.

They laughed as we struggled to keep the ladder upright. On more than one occasion, I thought we had lost it, and judging by the wail from the top of the ladder, so did Wolfy. Eventually, he had them all except for one pair of tattered old soccer shoes close to Grimley's bedroom window. "All of them," he sneered mockingly as we edged over the curb so Wolfy could reach. As Wolfy retrieved the last pair, it all went 'backside over breakfast,' as my Uncle Albert was fond of saying. Somehow, we had gotten front-heavy, and the momentum took us surging toward the house. However, there was a problem: the front wall. It was only three feet, but we had to stop or crash into it. Wolfy's momentum was pushing us on, and we were losing it, and possibly Wolfy. The ladder was now leaning heavily. There was no stopping it as it careened toward the house. Fortunately, big George somehow wedged himself between the ladder and the wall and stabilised everything. The only way now was to slowly lower Wolfy onto the roof of Grimley's front room bay window so he could safely step off and onto the top. Wolfy was safe. Furthermore, standing atop the bay window, Wolfy was only a yard from Grimley's open bedroom window. Wolfy climbed in.

It took a couple of minutes before Grimley realised what had happened. He rushed into the house, up the stairs, and emerged seconds later with Wolfy by the ear.

"I think this belongs to you," he said with the air of superiority that we had all come to know and despise.

"Let's go to the den," Billingsley suggested. So, we returned my dad's ladder and set off for the railway. Grimley, Nugent, and Paula were sitting on the front wall as we were leaving. "What a lot of schmucks," he yelled, laughing. "I don't know anyone who knows Mad Frankie Foster," he yelled after us, "Never did." We could hear them laughing as we headed out. We were dejected, and we sat around the den in silence until Beaky said what we were all thinking, "I hate that that oaf got the better of us." There was silence, then Wolfy spoke, "He didn't," he said quietly. We all looked at him inquiringly. "Wait until he goes to bed tonight and pulls the covers back," Wolfy said, breaking into a grin.

"You didn't?" I said.

"Yup," he said triumphantly. There was a moment of silence as we visualised Grimley pulling his sheets back later that night, and then we all laughed and laughed, and laughed. Revenge is indeed a dish best served on satin sheets.

All was well with the world that July. It was brightening by the minute, not only because the days were warm and sunny but because the big summer holiday was getting closer.

Eventually, a week later, the great day arrived. No more school for six weeks; it was true freedom. All that was left now was to hang out with the lads all summer and go on our big August family vacation. This year we were headed for France and as usual when the Brits cross the channel it often results in all-out war. This trip was no different.

August

Chapter 20
Holiday in France

By late summer 1968 we had come full circle, and the journal ended as it had begun. The last entry described in nine-year-old script was our family holiday to the Cote d'Azur. As I read through this last journal entry, I was taken back to that summer and the long car journey down through France to Provence and the Mediterranean Sea.

Once again, the dog days of August were upon us. They were as carefree as the white cotton ball clouds punctuating the bright blue skies above. I lazed on the warm grass, shielding my eyes from the bright summer sun. I knew that these days could not last and that soon September would come again as it always did, and we would be back at school, but not yet; not just yet. There was one last great adventure, our annual family summer holiday. This year, it would be the south of France, and I was very excited.

When I found out, I ran into the living room excited to tell my mother and brother where we were going for our holiday, but my brother immediately silenced me. Magdalen College, Oxford, was playing Birmingham University on the University Challenge quiz show, and my brother's hero, Bamber Gascoigne, the grand inquisitor, had just issued a starter for ten. My mother, who was fixing the curtains, informed me in a very low tone that the two competing colleges were, in what would be considered in football terms, the equivalent of extra time. I was momentarily stunned into silence by the fact that my mother had used a football analogy; this woman, I thought to myself, has unsuspected depth. I tried again to speak, but my brother silenced me with a reptilian-like hiss, which, coming from him, seemed almost natural. It was also accompanied by a malevolent stare, which directly translated from its undisguised hostility meant that terrible things would have resided in my future if I didn't shut my mouth.

I gazed frustratingly at the television set as some surly student from Birmingham, whose beard was so enormous he looked like he was chewing a cat, buzzed in to answer Bamber's question. The question was, "What was the name of the book published in 1947 by the famous Chinese phonetician that recorded patterns of speech in Western Manchuria and earned him a PhD?" This answer was for all the marbles, and the surly student hesitated momentarily before answering tentatively, "Doctor Hoo and the Dialects." "That is correct," moaned Bamber, the quiz master, less than enthusiastically and more than a little miffed that the 'great unwashed' of Birmingham had prevailed over the silver-tongued elite of Oxford.

The Oxfordians were now sobbing uncontrollably, presumably at the prospect of being debagged by those huge meaty rugger boys from Merton, after which they would receive a sound thrashing from the House Master, followed by a dose of castor oil from the matron and sent off to bed without supper. "No crumpets for them tonight," I yelled happily at my brother. His bottom lip was quivering as he had wanted those fellow geeks from Oxford to win.

Soon, it was "Cheerio" from Bamber, and I was finally allowed to speak. "I knew the answer to that question," my brother said haughtily. "You should," I said, "we watch it every Saturday afternoon after Grandstand." "What is it, dear?" my mother said, returning me from my strange daydream where David Coleman is a Time Lord. "Oh," I said, "yes, we are going to France on holiday; dad just told me," I said excitedly.

"We already knew that frog head," my brother replied, eagerly bursting my bubble. I was always the last to know everything. I had only just found out that Uncle Frank had been dead since 1964. I had been sending him a Christmas card posthumously for three years.

The week of the trip soon came and everyone in the house, except for my dad and me, were speaking French. My mother was practicing her French on our dog Hondo, named after my dad's favourite John Wayne movie. Hondo's lineage was somewhat questionable. A Heinz 57 mutt, he had a lopsided look due to an unnatural squint and a snarled lip. He had a vacant expression, which accurately reflected his diminished mental capabilities. His mother was a shameless hussy of a dog that lived three doors down and was of doubtful morals. He was the seventh of seven puppies, the runt that nobody wanted. I believe that his lopsided look, along with his snarly personality, diminished mental capacity, and lost and vacant expression, reminded my parents so much of my brother when he was little that they took Hondo out of sheer sentimentality.

Hondo understood only one word in English, which was 'food.' My mother's attempts to buy two tubes of lipstick and a yard brush from him in French fell on deaf ears. As if this wasn't bad enough, my brother came flouncing into the kitchen wearing a mauve-flowered shirt, orange pants, crepe-soled shoes, and more Brylcreem than a bar full of Teddy boys. To make matters worse, he was, for some strange reason, singing every third word of the current top ten hit, 'Yellow River.' He looked like the love child of Bill Haley and Liberace. My mother responded to his inquiry about how she was in French by replying, "Only on Tuesdays." My brother looked bemused and took off.

Uncle Norman was taking Hondo for the two weeks we were gone. There was much debate about this as the last time he returned from Uncle Norman's, he smelled of whiskey and would only answer to Glenfiddich. He took to sitting in front of my dad's drinks cabinet for hours on end, emitting an endlessly pathetic whimper. Nevertheless, it was decided that he should return to Uncle Norman's care for the duration.

We set off to France. This was a minor miracle, as only a few weeks earlier, I was in dire danger of joining Hondo at Uncle Norman's after a most unpleasant interlude. I returned home on the last day of school with my report card. My mother was in a remarkably good mood until she opened it. At that moment, all the good humour drained from her face, along with most of the blood. She took it from me with the look of a woman who had just received a summons from the Grim Reaper.

She opened it at arm's length, tilting her head way over her left shoulder as if her distant, straining sideways glance would somehow mitigate the horror of what was to come. She started to read it. I knew something was wrong when she gasped loudly and had to support herself against the kitchen table while my brother ran for the sherry. After a moment, she recovered enough to state, "Your father must not see this until after the summer holidays; we will enjoy a peaceful summer at least." She was calmer now and had stopped shaking, which meant more sherry was making it into the glass. Sadly, the hoped-for bliss of my dad's peaceful ignorance was not to be!

The previous November, I had given all the butterflies in my brother's prize collection a Viking's funeral by pinning them to bottle rockets on Bonfire night. I fired them off into the night sky on one last flight before they exploded into a thousand stars and entered Valhalla. In retaliation, my brother found my report card and showed it to my dad. This resulted in another explosion that lit the night sky. That was how I found myself back at school one evening the week after school was out for the summer.

I was most definitely in the proverbial doghouse. I found myself in a room with my teacher, the Headmaster, and my parents. The air was heavy with disdain, and I mean heavy; if looks could kill, I would have been dead more times than Captain Scarlet. They all began to discuss my abysmal academic record. It was bad enough that my mother had made me wear my school uniform, even though we were on summer break, but she had also made me sit on my hands because of my tendency to fidget. I was being discussed. Apparently, the rattling of Miss Collingwood's teacup and saucer on the desk, because of my continuously kicking the table leg, was getting on everyone's last collective nerve, so my mother tied my shoelace to the chair to force me to desist.

My teacher, Miss Collingwood began with my term project for geography, explaining that all the children had to do a project and present it to the class. She said the project I had chosen was "volcanic activity in the Isle of Man." She described, in horrifying detail, how, at my presentation, I disclosed my findings to the class in one short brief paragraph stating that because there are currently no volcanos on the Isle of Man, there was very little activity. She went on, warming to her task, by saying that I then produced a blank piece of paper with just two vertical and one horizontal line, "but nothing in between."

"Like his ears," muttered my father, just loud enough to receive a shushing from my mother. "Precisely," Miss Collingwood replied." This graph," she spat the word graph out like it left a bitter taste in her mouth, "is supposed to corroborate his statement by indicating the seismic activity south of Port Erin," she sighed, raising her hands in exasperation.

"Is that all he did?" my dad inquired.

"Not quite," Miss Collingwood said as she lowered her head and shook it in incredulous disbelief. She leaned down and produced a shoe box wrapped in tin foil, with the words written across the front, 'Volcanic rock from the Isle of Man.' There was a deep and mournful groan from my father, and my mother closed her eyes and sighed pitifully. They both knew what was coming. "There's nothing in that box, is there," my dad said pathetically. Miss Collingwood opened the lid to reveal brightly coloured tissue paper surrounding an empty spot in the middle with the words 'Lava rock from the Isle of Man'. She then remarked in a low, slow voice, punctuated with great deliberation, that the marks I received for the project were also directly equivalent to the amount of volcanic activity on the Isle of Man.

So, the endless night continued, and I wish I could say it got better, but it didn't. The sad story continued to unfold through maths, english, science, etc. Only in history had I shown any glimmer of hope when I had once named all the FA Cup winners since 1923. Eventually, after my mother had cried for the fourth time, they discussed how to remedy my academic malaise. Miss Collingwood and my mother were not in favour of my dad's solution of a damn good thrashing and urged a more scholarly and humane approach. My Headmaster, Mr Murdoch, suggested that I needed tutoring. I didn't like the sound of that. Half the dogs on our road had been tutored, and none of them were ever the same again. Eventually, they decided on extra homework through the holidays so that I could catch up on what I had so wantonly neglected during the term. I asked if I could have the damn good thrashing instead and was told, "No." I was also told not to swear; then, my mother started in on my dad for being a bad example.

The trip home was not a happy one. My dad's left eye had started twitching, and he was grinding his teeth. "Do you know how much I hate being dragged into that school room, sat in one of those little chairs, and have to listen to your teacher?" he yelled.

"Yes!" I replied, "Every day." It didn't help.

The days that followed were deeply reminiscent of a Dickens novel. I was forbidden friends, television, and dessert, except when my mother made rice pudding, I was forced to eat this as extra punishment. It reminded me a lot of my brother as it was very pale, had skin, and was quite thick. My dad had once used it to repair some tiles that had come loose in our bathroom. Eventually, I completed all the required work, including the school project, which was initially assigned by my dad, with the subject title: 'How lazy, indolent boys should never embarrass their fathers by being unbelievably stupid and should always be given a damn good thrashing whether they deserve it or not." but, my mother vetoed that, and I did one on Magpies instead.

As a reward, I escaped being sentenced to Uncle Norman's, and thus, I sat happily in the back of our car as we took off for parts unknown. When we began our journey, my mother decided we should speak French all the way to the Cote d'Azur. This was problematic, to say the least. My brother asked her for a bacon sandwich and received a washcloth. It wasn't long before we got lost, and I found out that my dad had some French words of his own. My mother seemed to understand these words and reproached him with her usual "Not in front of the children" pronounce-ment. I told her I had to go "Oui Oui" so she ordered my dad to pull over; he had more French words. I was beginning to think my dad was fluent.

There was nothing to read on the long journey south. There were my mother's romantic novels, with pictures of very healthy girls on the front cover and men with ponytails who had no shirt on while a storm raged in the background; no thanks. My brother's Wheat Growers Monthly was out of the question, so I read and reread my Beano annual, especially the Bash Street kids, who reminded me of the gang back home. Soon, we were heading south through Northern France. I asked my dad if we would see the Eiffel Tower, and he laughed and said only if there was a major navigating disaster, as our route took us on the ring road around the outskirts of Paris and on south.

The Eiffel Tower was awesome! My father had failed to consider my mother's navigational skills and her woeful sense of direction. I asked him later if what he said, as we went through the centre of Paris in all that traffic, was true about my mother getting lost on the way to our coal shed. The fact that my mother was communicating with him only through my brother gave me an inkling of her state of mind. By Lyon, my mother had moved from outright hostility to passive-aggressive disdain. By the time we reached Greno-ble, she had become cordially indifferent to him, and my brother stopped interpreting.

Soon, the magic of Provence began to cast its spell as we wove down through the Luberon. The soft and shifting light of the late afternoon coaxed and dispelled any darkness that lay upon the human heart, dissipating both resentment and pain in the purple hues of its gentle dusk. All the while, the scent of lavender filled the car with a rich sense of peace and well-being, which seemed to eclipse all moods and leave everyone with a perfect sense of hopeful anticipation.

It seemed all too soon that the Mediterranean came into view: blue and grand, she spread herself before us. Billingsley had informed me before we left, that the Med was very big and very blue, and you couldn't miss it. If you sailed into the middle of it, you would come to the Isle of Wight.

We arrived in Cap d'Antibes and checked into our awesome hotel. My brother and I shared a room. The room was amazing, and the bathroom had both a toilet and a drinking fountain right next to it! We played on the beach for two whole weeks, swam in the sea, and ate things that lived in the pond at the bottom of our garden. I drank Orangina mostly and Stella Artois when my dad wasn't looking. My dad didn't have an overly good opinion of the French when we began the holiday. That attitude didn't improve as he engaged in a war of attrition over those two weeks with the hotel waiter assigned to our table, whom he insisted on calling garçon, or 'boy' in English. He had always said that he thought the French were the most evenly balanced people in the world because they had a chip on both shoulders. This sentiment did not endear him when he retold it to Francois, our waiter.

Francois was a big, burly, thick-chested man with a large nose and an easy grin. He had a huge moustache, thinning hair, and a florid complexion; he looked like a sergeant of Napoleon's Imperial Guard. He liked me. He would ruffle my hair and say, "Ça va Jimmy?" every morning while he poured my orange juice and tossed me a chocolate croissant. Francois smiled at my mother and brother but scowled at my dad, who ignored him. That was until his coffee cup wasn't refilled. At this point, he growled at the big Frenchmen, who reluctantly refilled it while muttering French obscenities under his breath. My dad retaliated by speaking only in English colloquialisms and refusing to tip him.

Consequently, my father never had any eggs on his plate, and his coffee was only ever lukewarm. My dad insisted on marmalade every morning, yet somehow only received Nutella, a French nutty chocolate concoction that infuriated my father no end. This went on for a week, which my mother declared intolerable in her less-than-perfect French. It was then that the miracle of Cap d'Antibes happened.

It happened at the end of the first week, when my mother had retired early, and my dad, by all accounts, had remained in the bar for a drink. Apparently, Francois had also come in on his night off for a drink. The two sat across the bar, eyeing each other warily.

"Bonsoir Rosbif," said Francois insultingly.

"Evening Frog," replied my father, not to be outdone. The evening progressed from trading insults to trading drinks until they were both very drunk. During their conversation, it turned out that Francois' and my father's units had fought side by side together in the Ardennes during the Battle of the Bulge. What happened next becomes a bit vague, as it did involve the two of them sitting at the fountain in the town square at midnight, singing "Lilly Marlene" at the top of their voices. It took a gendarme, the hotel manager, and my mother in curlers and bathrobe to restore order.

My dad didn't appear the next morning, and we had a different waiter for breakfast. The upshot of what my dad called the 'Bon Accord' was that they became inseparable, and we dined at Francois' house one glorious summer evening in the foothills north of the town. We were served cuisine Provincial, washed down with copious amounts of Rhone wine. Francois watered down a glass of wine and let me drink with everyone else. My mother was less than convinced, obviously picturing her son in some dark future sitting under a motorway bridge in rags, sipping methylated spirits out of an old Billy can while begging for money to get home from Barnsley. There I was, under the grape arbour, around that great stone family table, happily sipping wine legitimately for the first time as the shifting light gilded the distant blue enamel sea with her golden caress. That night, we drank wine and drew the last heat from the day. And as the twilight turned purple on the far dusk-streaked horizon, I fell in love with France.

The journey home was incident-free for the most part, except for when my brother got caught in the new self-cleaning toilets just north of Chalon and smelled of detergent all the way back to Manchester. The only dark cloud on a clear and serene horizon that late August as we made our way back through the hinterland of France was that the start of yet another school year was now only a matter of days away. And so, the last journal entry came to a close as the last cloudless days of August ebbed away. The school year 1967-68 had come and gone in a blur of nonstop activity that I later would come to recognise as life.

Epilogue

━━━◆○◆━━━

Where are they now

Cynthia Hardcastle continued to be a goddess among lesser mortals for many years. She grew up if it were possible to be even more beautiful than any of us dreamed of or anticipated. At eighteen, she was Captain of the village women's tennis team and drew more crowds than Wimbledon. It was not surprising that so many boys now in their late teens who had known and adored her as young kids still sat and watched her play on Saturday mornings, with their tongues dragging the baseline as wide-eyed and twitter-pated as they had been all those years before. Eventually, she married and moved to the wield of Kent, where they bought a house and had two daughters who, I am sure, tormented a whole new generation of feckless boys.

Wolfy and I remain great friends. He moved away with his parents soon after leaving junior school, eventually settling in the Lake District. He still lives and works there as a painter and decorator. Somehow, it is not surprising that he would spend so much of his life at the top of a ladder, having survived being on top of the one held by the ten of us. The Rugby ball sits on top of a vast filing cabinet, and we often talk about those adventures. It must just be habit or nostalgia that I always look in the bottom drawer of that cabinet, but there is never a cat in it.

My brother experienced a great metamorphosis two years later. By the time he was sixteen, he frightened everyone by becoming very athletic. He became an accomplished goalkeeper at football, playing for both his local club and his works team. He also became a proficient fast bowler, starring for our village under eighteens XI. Extraordinary as it might sound, people actually started to like him, including me, which surprised everyone. He was especially popular with the girls after he finally discovered where their lips were. This transformation into a tough, rugged, macho man's man was completed in later life. He became a shift supervisor. He also became a champion darts player. He no longer batters me as he once did, which is a great relief at family reunions. He married a lovely local girl with whom he shares an extensive family. I have long believed that the change was due to the *Mysterons*.

My Parents were very happily married for well over half a century until my mother sadly passed away. She never learned to drive. They exemplified all that was good. They were always there for us, as constant as the North Star, that one fixed point in an ever-changing world.

Mugger Murdoch, our Headmaster, whom we came to know so well, is still alive and living in our village. Even now, when I see him in the village, he offers to cane me, suggesting with a rye smile that I probably have done something to deserve it. Miss Collingwood eventually married, raised three children, and lives somewhere in Cornwall.

The Gang: Limpy became a plumber and lived in the midlands somewhere near Birmingham. Beaky became an electrical engineer and is happily married with two grown children. We are all happy that his engineering career didn't include building boats. Billingsley sadly passed away in 2007. Later in life, he was a journalist for our local paper.

His grasp of the facts improved drastically and were distinctly more accurate than when he was young, much to the relief of the entire community.

Snowy works for the BBC, which explains a lot. Mikey still lives in the area and works for the local council. I often visit him when I am home, usually during his three-hour lunch break. We reminisce and drink terrible local government coffee. Ginger emigrated to Australia, lives near the WACA in Perth, and never misses a test match. Frothy moved, and we never heard from him again. Cockney still lives in Manchester, but these days, when it comes to girls, he is nowhere near as afflicted as he used to be.

Big George became a greengrocer and owned a small shop just outside the village for many years. He is retired and is President of the local bowling club. He still refuses to go to the cinema with me to this day.

The Others: Jumbo Butterworth grew up to own a chain of fish and chip shops in Blackburn and Burnley, which were very successful. He made a bundle and retired early to live in Jersey, where he enjoys the good life. Paula Postlethwaite now regrets not marrying Jumbo. Instead, she became a professional show jumper and toured the world; it is said that no fence she ever faced would ever dare dislodge itself. Ronald Marchbanks became a successful salesman who sold corporate insurance and lives in London. Tiny Teddy Fothergill eventually grew up, but not by much. I believe he still takes his booster seat to Old Trafford where he never misses a game. Lenny Farris was a mechanic and worked at Trafford Park for many years, before retiring to Bournemouth. I believe that he has finally learned that peanuts are much less annoying and much more pleasant when you put them in your mouth. Talky still lives in East Texas with his beautiful wife and four children.

Georgie Lightfoot became a clothes designer and buyer for Marks and Spencer's. He still has his superpower to this day.

All the Miss Chambers, with the possible exception of already possibly dead Miss Chambers, as well as Farmer Newton and Sergeant Steele, are all long gone, as is the great and much-loved Peter, our butcher, who coached us to our epic victory on the green all those years ago. Mr Balinsky, our school caretaker still lives in the old caretaker's house by the school. By my math, he is about 156 years old...could he really be Father Christmas? More than likely, it's just my terrible arithmetic, which has not improved much since 1968.

Liverpool. In the years to come, I visited Liverpool many times and have come to consider it one of my favourite cities. I have many friends there and was, in time, able to overcome the traditional rivalry and animosity that exists between the two cities. I even went to Anfield, and yes, I got well within fifty yards of the Mersey and I don't glow in the dark.

As for Bolton Wanderers, well, they have gone missing again.

As for me, well, I still remember all of the boys of '68. We were an unlikely brotherhood, forged by fire and bonded by memory. We will always share that brief moment in time when, for us, the world was young, and the path of life yet remained untrodden. Somewhere out there at the end of boyhood, we would find that path, the one that was always waiting to take us all on a much grander and infinitely more wondrous adventure.

Printed in Dunstable, United Kingdom